GIVE ME SHELTER

An Irishman's Struggle to Become the
Seven Summits World Record Holder

Ian McKeever

BLACKWATER PRESS

Editor
Claire Rourke

Design & Layout
Paula Byrne

Cover Design
Karen Hoey

ISBN 978-1-84741-188-4

© Ian McKeever, 2007

Produced in Ireland by
Blackwater Press
c/o Folens Publishers
Hibernian Industrial Estate
Tallaght
Dublin 24

Contents

Climbing timeline

Five Peaks world record, 25 June 2004

Croagh Patrick seven times in seventeen hours, 25 June 2005

100-hour challenge across the 26 peaks of Britain and Ireland, 21–24 June 2006

2007 Seven Summits timeline

Depart Ireland, 6 January

Summit Vinson, 25 January

Leave Antarctica, 30 January

Arrive on Aconcagua, 4 February

Summit Aconcagua, 11 February

Off the mountain, 14 February

Arrive in Africa, 26 February

Summit Kilimanjaro, 5 March

Arrive in Indonesia, 12 March

Summit Carstensz pyramid, 16 March

Depart for Russia, 2 April

Failed Elbrus bid, 9 April

Arrive base camp Everest, 23 April

Summit Everest, 16 May

Arrive back in Russia, 28 May

Summit Elbrus, 30 May

Arrive Alaska, 10 June

Summit Denali, 29 June

Arrive Australia, 5 July

Summit Snowy Mountain, 11 July

Acknowledgements

Records are made to be broken:

Record number one: Seven Summits in a time of 155 days, beating the old record by 32 days.

Record number two: Alternative Seven Summits in a time of 169 days, beating the old record by 2 days.

My incredible journey taught me that there is no such thing as 'ordinary' but only the extraordinary potential that lies within all of us. Setting this inspiring, but challenging, word record and getting to write about it in this book could not have been possible without a great deal of courage and support from those whose faith in me for which I am forever indebted.

I would like to thank the following:

John O'Connor and the incredible staff at Blackwater Press, my publisher, for having faith in me.

Claire Rourke, my editor, for turning this into a book.

My book sponsors Vivas Health, whose core motto teaches us to empower ourselves.

Caoimhe Buckley for her thankless hours of research.

The teaching staff at Clonkeen College. 'Tada gan iarracht' ('Nothing without effort'), as they say.

My parents for their continued love and support.

All my friends, most especially Cathal Cregg, Aisling Forkin, Ciara Scott, Ann Healy, Dymphna O'Brien, Grainne Walsh, Lorraine McGovern, Dave Burke, Brenda Burke and Eugene Grey for always believing and never judging me.

David Pritt for making the journey possible.

John Whittle of *Touching the Void*, whose vision will paint an everlasting picture.

Ulster Bank, Berghaus and Maximuscle for their wonderful support in rising with me to the challenge.

Dietician Orla Duffy and John Baldwin of La Sante Health store whose wisdom taught me we are what we absorb!

Dr Shane Murnaghan, who taught me that to truly heal a person you must first raise their spirit.

Des Macken and Enda McNulty, who made that all important 1 per cent in the difference.

Dedication

This book is dedicated to those who inspire us in life.
For Maire, who taught me 'the dance'.

Preface

John Morrison and Oliver Tattan at Kala Pathar, Everest Base Camp.

Ian McKeever and I first met while training for the Five Peaks Challenge in 2000. Ian struggled up Djouce Mountain in Wicklow one Saturday morning with a hangover, a thermos flask of coffee and a packet of cigarettes which he shared around liberally. We were part of a mixed group organised by John Morrison to do a fundraising and record-breaking attempt on the five highest mountains in Britain and Ireland. Ian ultimately caved on Slieve Donard, the second mountain. I knew he had been a sprinter at school, and, smokes aside, endurance walks seemed new territory to him. Four of us finished in less than 42 hours, a new surface record at the time.

In 2004 after a change in lifestyle and disciplined health-management program, Ian would return to complete the Five Peaks – with air transport this time– in just over 16 hours, still an unbroken world record. Nevertheless in December 2006, when Ian told me of his Seven Summits Challenge, I was sceptical. To take on one of the most gruelling high altitude endurance challenges in the world, when he had only experienced air as thick as pea soup on the hillocks of Ireland, seemed a bigger bite than even he would be able to chew. The plan was to climb Mount Vinson in Antarctica, Aconcagua in South America, Kilimanjaro in Africa, Carstensz Pyramid in Australasia, Mount Elbrus in Europe and Mount Everest in Asia. When he set out shortly afterwards, I never considered an eventuality whereby he might match Canadian Daniel Griffith's record of 187 days. In fact, he returned victorious, knocking an incredible thirty-two days off the world record, bringing it down to 155 days.

In *Give Me Shelter*, Ian tells the story of that challenge and achievement. His story is of an ordinary guy, who, with dedication and perseverance came, good against huge physiological, psychological, topological, meteorological and organisational challenges. A story of how, with focused management of his health, fitness and confidence, he came to take control of his own performance. Ian tells us a very human story of his own personal journey and of the people he met along the way.

It is also a chronicle of exhaustion and euphoria, despair and victory which will ring true to anyone who has ever pushed themselves too far and wished just to give up, to sit and sleep awhile – a sleep from which, when taken at altitude, there is no awakening. We all face our own form of high-altitude challenges in life. *Give Me Shelter* is the story of one man who summoned the focus, courage and stamina to achieve his dream and rank him as one of the great Irish adventurers of our time. Enjoy.

Oliver Tattan, CEO of VIVAS Health
November 2007

Prologue
No Way Out

'Ability is of little account without opportunity.'
Napoleon Bonaparte

'Is it just pressure, Ian, or actual pain that you are feeling?' he asked.

What do you think? I screamed to myself, but instead chose to mumble, 'Jesus, Tony, that's killing me!'

When I was younger, I never had a problem with the dentist's chair. Perhaps that's because I never went enough – even though the whole experience of having your teeth removed or going under the anaesthetic can hold a strange appeal to a twelve year old with a vivid imagination. It makes perfect schoolyard material to embellish and gloat cheerfully about to the lads on a chilly morning. This was different. It was 23 December 2006, I was thirty-six, sitting in Dr Tony Connellan's chair, waiting to have the last of my molars removed from the upper right side of my mouth. I was stranded in the salubrious surrounds of Dublin's Rathgar Road in Rathmines, scared in a way I couldn't even bring myself to comprehend.

It was 10.30 a.m. precisely. I remember because I could hear Radio 1 on in the background. Pat Kenny had just linked to the ads. They are very precise on Radio 1. Despite working in communications for fifteen years – nearly all of my professional life – to this day, and to my embarrassment, I couldn't (with one notable exception) name any of the presenters after 7 p.m. on our national broadcaster. As I sat there in the dentist's chair, however, I couldn't help but think that most people on this green isle of ours who tune into radio, over 90 per cent of the population in fact, would probably enjoy debating the thought running through my mind. Why is it, I would ask, that you mysteriously wake up one morning (you must have celebrated at least your thirtieth birthday, mind) and find yourself inadvertently switching on the country's flagship news and currents affairs programme *Morning Ireland?* It's as if you suddenly feel guilty for spending your entire life uninformed.

The tension inside me was palpable, 'I've never seen you like this, Ian', Tony said, with genuine concern in his voice. I was starting to drift in and out of making sense (seven shots of anaesthetic to calm the pressure and pain will do that to you). I could feel my entire body tensing and I was gripping anything I could get hold of, including squeezing the blood from the poor dental nurse's hand. I was spitting blood and I thought at that very moment, as Dr Connellan twisted the gripping device even tighter, that the entire right side of my brain was about to merge with my few remaining teeth. Tony was afraid that we had run out of time. We were clean out of options and there was no time now to consider root canal. This was safer...

❀❀❀

My mind began drifting once more... *Christ, what the hell was I actually doing?*

Why even contemplate trying to undertake the Seven Summits Challenge – something that less than 160 people in this world had ever managed to achieve? Let alone want to make the first ever documentary of it, a documentary that was going to potentially leave me broke for the rest of my life and with even greyer hair?

Typical McKeever, I thought, *always thinking up the impossible!* That somehow all my ducks would just line up all by themselves and, hey presto, I'd be able not only to climb each of the continents' highest peaks, and, oh yeah, I was gong to do it faster than anyone else for a new world record *and* document the whole experience no matter how much it was all going to cost me or what effect it would have on those I loved! Richard Attenborough meets Chris Bonnington – just how much anaesthetic was I under?

At least, the thinking behind the documentary was noble; capturing the varying topographies of each of these incredible peaks, while at the same time revealing the often forgotten rich cultures behind the mountains; rare insights into tribes like the Danni in Indonesia and the famous Masai in Tanzania. I mean, to think that no one had thought of it before, beggared belief, right? Aquarians are born dreamers after all...

The actual record for the fastest completion of the Seven Summits on the seven continents finished in November 2006 and was held by a highly engaging professional Canadian climber in his early fifties named Daniel Griffiths.

His version of the challenge included the highest peak in Australasia, a tough testing peak called Carstenez Pyramid that stands just under 5,000 metres and is located deep in the heart of the Papuan jungle in Indonesia.

The alternative version of the challenge included Snowy Mountain, or Kosciuszko, located a pleasant six hours by car, south of Sydney in Australia. This mountain was more of a giant hill (it stands at 2,600 metres), requiring no technical aids and was favoured of a Sunday afternoon by healthy Australians. The record for this version, an impressive 172 days, was held by an interesting if rather odd Indian character known to simple Westerners like me as Mabu.

It was Richard Bass, an American businessman and amateur mountaineer, who first set himself the goal of climbing the highest mountain on each of the seven continents, including mainland Australia. He hired the talented mountaineer David Breashears to guide him up Everest, regarded then as the most difficult of his seven. Bass completed his Everest summit on 30 April 1985 and then co-authored the book *Seven Summits,* which covered his undertaking. Reinhold Messner, the brilliant Italian climber, revised Bass' list by substituting the Australia-New Guinea continent with mainland Australia. Pat Morrow first met Messner's challenge, finishing with climbing Carstensz Pyramid on 7 May 1986, shortly followed by

Messner himself climbing Vinson in the Antarctic (the first mountain I would face), on 3 December 1986.

Morrow was the first to complete all eight summits from both lists. He modestly suggested that the only reason that he beat Messner was because Messner was also busy getting through the fourteen highest peaks over 8,000 metres.

In 1990, Rob Hall and Gary Ball became the first to complete the Seven Summits in seven months, raising the bar to a whole new level, bringing the intensity associated with a speed challenge that required supreme mental and physical stamina. Using the Bass list, they started with Mount Everest on 10 May 1990 and finished with Vinson on 12 December, with just hours before the seven-month deadline would have expired. The first woman to complete the Bass and Messner lists was Junko Tabei, who finished on 28 July 1992, having stood proudly on the summit of Europe's highest peak, Elbrus.

It's worth pointing out that when I decided to undertake this world record attempt on 8 November 2005, I'd never been above the height of Ben Nevis, Scotland's tallest mountain and the highest peak in the British Isles standing at 1,300 metres. But something inside told me that the principle of placing one foot in front of the other might actually be enough to enable me to step outside my comfort zone and try something this spectacular, this wild and adventurous. This was the ultimate challenge of mind and body. Sure, I could have done a tough marathon, or even tried to train for a whole series, but the reality was I needed something that would test and fulfil me in every possible way – mentally, physically and spiritually, mind and body in motion, over a sustained and prolonged period. I needed to go, as one Captain James T. Kirk might have put it, where no man had gone before.

A curious call to David Pritt, managing director of Adventure Peaks (a UK company located in the Lake District that specialises in such bizarre expeditions) followed that very morning.

'Let me get this straight,' David said. 'You want to smash the world record by climbing the Seven Summits in less than 180 days, doing both Carstenez Pyramid in Indonesia and Snowy Mountain in Australia if you make it that far – eight summits just for good measure. You want to do this having never been to altitude, having never rock climbed and having never stepped foot on ice and–'

'Sorry to interrupt, Dave. The other thing is that I need to start in twelve months' time, no later! No, I haven't confirmed the sponsor just yet, but if you could email me a possible schedule for the record attempt, together with the required training programme for the mountains that I'll need to undertake over the coming months – that would be really great. Oh and, by the way, I'm meeting with Ulster Bank in two days, so if you could advise approximate costs for that meeting…'

I believe the scene that followed in the Adventure Peaks staff room could be roughly recreated as, 'Did you hear the one about the Paddy who had no money and thought he'd break the record for the Seven Summits by climbing eight mountains!' A great deal of laughter ensued, naturally!

To Dave Pritt's eternal credit, he forwarded all of the details as requested and within twenty-four hours. Dave had been brought up in the heart of Cumbria, from a working-class background, and from a very early age it had been instilled in this man to respect what he had and work hard for the things he didn't.

Though there would be many changes and alterations to the document that Dave sent me, his email gave me the details I needed to set about achieving my dream and set in motion a chain of events that were irreversible.

However, so many difficult challenges had faced me coming into Dr Connellan's dental chair that it's really no wonder that I needed the same sedation as a fully grown horse! My body had gone through the literal mill, between training injuries, a shattering training schedule and impossibly challenging diet needs. But, for all of that, it was the immense financial pressure that was now finally taking its toll on me. I had set myself a seemingly impossible challenge and, although I had secured personal support from Ulster Bank, I had only a matter of hours to come up with another STG£40,000-plus to get my cameraman a guaranteed place on the flight to the Antarctic, to enable us to make this documentary that everyone said couldn't be made...

At the end of November, I sat down with my accountant, John Nolan, a brilliant and generous man, and we talked about my dream of making the documentary and my need to borrow personally to provide the finance. I needed a professional proposal for my own bank, Bank of Ireland. But, of course, given the short timescale to the beginning of the challenge in early January 2007, time was of the essence. In my accountant's mind, it was simply vital that a video record was made of the attempt. But his experience told him that, given the unique nature of the undertaking, the proposal to the bank had to be comprehensive and impressive enough to win their support. So, John burned the candles at both ends to produce a business plan which we both felt gave the proposal the best possible chance of succeeding.

It was now getting close to Christmas and, as anybody in business in Ireland will tell you, that it is about the worst time of year to try to get anything done, especially getting a bank to approve funding for any project. I knew we were up against it time-wise and I also knew that security would be an issue. John had told me that he felt we were likely to need either someone to put up cash or to act as guarantor for the borrowings and he suggested that I circulate the plan to any wealthy friends I had.

The bank reacted very positively to the proposal but, as I suspected, needed a guarantor or some cash injection. But, it soon became clear to us that a guarantor was not going to be secured in time. However, I had mentioned that I might be able to get some people to put up amounts of maybe €5,000 each to help, so John redrafted the proposal to aim it at non-corporate investors. He suggested setting up a company to facilitate any investment and this was when Take Me Higher Limited was born.

I now had three hours to make this idea work and to find people to pledge amounts of €5,000 albeit we were looking to raise at least €80,000. Dave Pritt would be phoning me at exactly 5 p.m. Irish time from the foothills of the Antarctic, where he was guiding another client group, in anticipation of our arrival — and it was going to take at least an hour for the swelling in my mouth to go down so that I could talk properly… Wasn't I lucky that a day has few hours but an extravagance of minutes and a multitude of seconds? I was going to need to make every single one of them count like they had never counted before.

1

The Wonder Years

*'Heaven lies about us in our infancy and the world begins
lying about us pretty soon afterward.'*

Ambrose Bierce

As adults, we sometimes marvel at the innocence of children. We
continuously crave that sensation of experiencing everything as if it's
for the first time. However, as much as we occasionally wish to be
transported back to our youth, we nevertheless disdain one attribute
held in alarmingly equal measure by so many children: their capacity
to be cruel.

I have very few early childhood memories – only two in fact:
sipping Harp out of my Aunt Pamela's glass and collecting my sister
Denise from the hospital when I was almost three years of age. That
first taste of Harp occurred in Donegal when I was four.

My father's best friend at the time, Cyril Winder, lived just outside
Dunloe with his wife Eithne and their three children in the rather aptly
named 'Little Bridge House'. This quaint but splendid home
overlooked a gorgeous lake with wonderful views that, at the time,
had, thankfully, very few dwellers on either side. It was a truly beautiful
place to spend summers, playing with Rusty their dog, swimming in the
lake or going on long cycles around the peninsula.

Dad and Cyril had been friends since their schooldays in Belvedere
College. Cyril was one of the great characters, known the length and

breath of Donegal. Professionally, he ran the co-op shops (founded originally by Pat the Cope himself) which stood as famously and proudly as any landmarks you might care to mention at the time. Cyril had a wicked sense of humour and often played tricks with the local customers. He was as shrewd as he was kind and no trip to Dunloe would ever be complete without a visit to the local co-op store. Cyril smoked like a trooper and was fond of a tipple or two but, whenever he was in the room, there was always a great sense of joy and wonderment. My father and mother loved him dearly, as did I.

In 1974 – the year I drank the Harp – my Uncle Oliver and his wife Pamela had come to join us in Donegal. As it happened, Cyril and his family were spending that particular summer in Dublin. Oliver had worked hard to build up his own taxi and courier business in Watford, just outside London, and had come to take a well-earned break, joining Mum and Dad in Donegal. My mother, who was also English, was very close to Oliver and Pamela and when it comes to getting on with my father, well you'd have to be made out of stone not to like my father Niall, or Neil as his family still calls him today. He has this undeniably dry sense of humour which is infectious once you get him going.

Every holiday in Donegal always finished with a trip to Burtonport, just north of Dunloe, to stock up on salmon steak, which was to be stored in those exceptionally long freezers (which every family seemed to have back then) throughout the winter. Perhaps that's where my love affair with fish began. In later years, when I was to go back to serious physical training, I could often be seen leaving the local Spar in Roundwood, County Wicklow, with a week's supply of up to twenty cans of John West tuna fish drenched in sunflower oil (I hope they never test my mercury levels).

❦❦❦

My sister was a very cute baby. Like most loving brothers I tortured her at first... leaving her for hours on end in her playpen with no toys to play with.

For the first ten to twelve years or so, it would be fair to say my sister Denise and I were actually very close. We did most things together and I took great pride when I grew a little older in looking out for her, whether it was just going to the shops or enjoying our first family holiday abroad in Majorca in 1980, when we learned to play the maracas together.

In 1982, we got to take a second foreign holiday together, this time behind the great Iron Curtain. We were on holiday in Romania, a country that, at the time, was in a state of complete flux. Ceauşescu remained in power and Romanians remained far from equal. Dollar shops dotted the port of Constantia, where we were staying, as plentifully as the number of sailors who came ashore to sell sexual favours in return for pairs of Levi jeans. Every morning, you couldn't but wonder at the number of sunburned Westerners going into the shops. They were mostly female. At the time, I just figured that jeans must be better and cheaper in Romania! I had much to learn. The Iron Curtain was finally opening its drapes to the commercial greed of the West.

I had made two good friends on that particular holiday. There was Liam who hailed from Manchester, a very tubby but charming twelve year old, who bubbled over with surprising energy, and Magdalena, a stunning looking fourteen year old, originally from Bucharest who had fled south several years earlier with her younger brother, Leon, and their father, who was a doctor.

For the most part, we used to spend our days happily out in the sea, playing innocently together as a group of kids should, basking in the warm sunshine.

The food was awful, consisting on certain evenings of not more than raw cabbage with vinegar dressing. I thank my lucky stars to this day that, over those entire fourteen days, we were never hit with an almighty dose of the runs that crippled most of the occupants in the hotel where we were staying.

There wasn't much to buy outside the dollar shops locally, save the odd hand-carved chessboard, but I remember the Romanian people were a delight to be around. It was the first time I'd spent any kind of real time around a culture other than my own, and it gave me a valuable insight into how people could be genuinely happy with really very little to shout about in terms of material wealth or the type of personal freedoms that you and I take for granted. It wasn't till many years later when I spent time in Brno, in the Czech Republic, that I came to have a full understanding of what life under the Communists must have been like.

That holiday in Romania stands out in my mind for two reasons. It was the last one that we ever took as a family abroad and, more importantly, it gave me the opportunity to spend quality time with my family, most especially with Dad, to whom I was very close. All the girlfriends I've ever had will testify to the fact that my old man is really pretty cool – to paraphrase Dickens from Great Expectations, he's 'not only a gentleman but a gentle man'.

Dad has a quirky sense of humour. I'll always remember queuing patiently with the masses outside McDonald's when they opened their first restaurant in Dún Laoghaire, not far from Cabinteely, where we were living at the time. It was 1980 and everyone wanted a Big Mac. I was salivating at the prospect. However, when it came to finally placing the order Dad decided that it was illogical that people would serve two burgers inside one bun and so we settled for a hamburger and chips instead.

Dad was always fascinated with the grunts that Jimmy Connors used to make as we sat enthralled every summer watching Wimbledon. Mum couldn't contain her delight in 1977 when a nerve-ridden Virginia Wade finally clawed past a bewildered Betty Stova to give England it's coveted prize in the Queen's Silver Jubilee year.

Whatever about Connors' grunt, it was the length of time that it took McEnroe to serve that really wound Dad up. But then, as if in response, to the audacity of guys like Connors and McEnroe, he'd ask, 'Why do professional tennis players need two serves anyway? Surely one's enough if they're getting paid!' It was my mum, though, who engendered in me a love of sport and decent music, like the Mamas and Papas and Aretha Franklin, from an early age. I became your typical sport Billy who knew the words to songs, and who made most guys my age look at me as if I had arrived on this planet before the Mods had even had the chance to take over.

I guess it was sometime in between eating my first hamburger and watching Italy deny a gifted Brazilian team the World Cup in 1982, that I learned that I was adopted. Or at least that's when I became aware that I was different to the other kids that I knew in the neighbourhood. The nuns from St Patrick's Guild, where my parents had gone through the adoption process, would, of course, have paid regular visits to our home when we were young kids to check that all was in order, but such visits held little or no significance for me.

The summer of 1982 was also when my skin began to change horribly and my voice sounded strangely deeper to those who rang when I picked up the telephone. That World Cup was also the one with Northern Ireland's famous, wonderful victory over the host nation Spain, the eternal underachievers in the competition. Even at an early age, I always felt a connection with the green jersey. It never mattered to me, whether it was NI or ROI. The fact was it was green. There I was cheering them on, voice breaking in a very serious way, and bristles looming on my spotty chin.

I had come back from Romania with a great tan but was now about to start secondary school with a face full of yellow spots. 'What the hell is happening to me?' I knew how Peter Parker must have felt before he changed into Spider-Man! Coinciding with the move to Clonkeen College, there was a move of home. We didn't move far, from Cabinteely to neighbouring Killiney, but the difference in the size of the house was considerable. My parents had bought a house in an estate adjacent to my old primary school, Johnstown NS. Watson's Nurseries used to be on the land on which the estate was built, and it was transformed into perfect suburbia; a series of connecting roads, each with its own distinct style of modern home. We were on Watson Road in a four-bed detached house. Dad had worked hard to get us there.

All of my close mates from primary school lived nearby, which was comforting as a twelve year old who walked most places.

I had decided one evening to gather the crew together to discuss being adopted as it was starting to really make me feel different form the rest of the lads. Trust me, when you're twelve, the last thing you want to be is different in any way, shape or form.

At this point, I should perhaps remind you all about being twelve years of age. If, as a kid, you have what you perceive to be a serious problem, you can go one of two routes. Bottle it or share it. I preface the following comments by admitting that I am not a parent, but I think the worst thing a kid can do is bottle his or her emotions.

It never ceases to amaze me how little some parents actually know about what's going on when it comes to their children. Kids experience a whole spectrum of emotions that, sadly, parents can sometimes not appreciate – particularly in today's world of technological and communication advancements. Ironic, don't you think?

If, like me, you decide to share your emotions with your mates, the one thing you probably bank on more than anything else is a degree of empathy. Of course, at twelve, it never dawned on me that because I was the only one in the group who was adopted, it was going to be difficult, at best, for my friends to understand my plight.

'Do your real parents know where you are?' piped up Conor, one of my best mates from primary school.

'Actually, I don't know who they are,' I admitted, feeling rather like I was in the local confessional with Fr Mangan, our local curate.

'Shouldn't somebody tell them where you are?' said Rob, who lived just around the corner.

'Must be weird for your parents,' said another.

'Yeah, but it must be weirder for you, Ian. You don't even know why your real mother left you. How weird is that? '

The group were now in unison. I felt like I was imploding. 'I don't know, lads,' I replied, desperation in my voice. 'I don't know anything. I just know my parents said I was even more special because they chose me and I'm adopted.' Before I could take back the words they were out – God, how I would regret those utterances. In the eyes of some of those twelve year olds, I had just tried to elevate my position within the group.

I knew they thought I was saying I was above them. But to their credit, they said nothing. It was Conor who had the good sense to break up the so-called 'meeting' by declaring that it was getting late.

It was several weeks in fact before I felt the full fallout from my words. I'll never forget walking out of church one Sunday. There was a group of lads gathered across the road, as if lying in wait for me. I recognised one or two of them, several older brothers of my friends among them. 'Ladies and gentlemen, it's Mr Adopted himself – he's so special. Everyone thinks so except his real birth parents, of course.'

It was the one and only time I would allow myself to cry in public.

❧❧❧

I guess if you asked most people about their school years, some would moan and groan, others would shrug their shoulders, but then there would always be the circumspect few whose faces would light up at the prospect of recounting those formative years.

I was really lucky to have had a wonderful primary-school education, which set me up nicely, I felt, for what might lie ahead. One of my favourite teachers from those distant primary days was a gentleman by the name of Niall O'Neil. He wore his hair typically long for the period in question – late 1970s – and he had thick-rimmed glasses. Apart from being a superb teacher (we were lucky to have him for fifth and sixth class), he also took us for sports as he was in charge of the Johnstown school soccer team. Niall knew soccer like the back of his hand, having had trials for Liverpool at the end of the 1960s. He was generous with his time and his expertise. We had our little Robbie Keane back then, a guy by the name of Roger Dunne, small like Robbie but lightning quick. Every match day, his mum (the carbon copy of Julie Walters), who was our local lollipop lady, used to give us preferential treatment crossing the road! We won one league championship and lost a cup final under the man who would have played for Liverpool.

The next time our paths crossed was at the 1982 Christmas fair, which was held in Johnstown girl's school next door to ours. I was down bargain hunting for Christmas presents for the folks when Niall, who was there, I recall, playing Santa in the grotto, called me over, 'Hey, Mr McKeever, aren't you going to say hello?' His deep gravelly voice carrying fifty metres at least. He could see that I was nervous approaching the grotto. 'What's happened to your face?' he said, 'Why are you wearing brown foundation? You're not in the Christmas panto, are you?'

I was glad the foundation was covering the fact that my cheeks were turning bright red. How was I going to explain to him why I was wearing make-up? How was I going to explain it to myself for that matter? My skin was covered with pustular acne and I was so ashamed of the way I looked. My self-image was really poor and I was struggling more than ever to come to terms with finding out that I was adopted. The make-up was my mask, my protection from the world, so that I didn't have to explain anymore why I was different. 'Sorry, Mr O'Neill, I have to go. Please excuse me.' What must he have thought? The bright-eyed, outgoing goalkeeper he knew was gone and, in his place, there was a timid and shy kid on the cusp of turning thirteen, already fraught with insecurities.

2

I Should Have Been at School

'You are educated when you have the ability to listen to almost anything without losing your temper or self-confidence.'

Robert Frost

Growing up in 1980s Ireland was not easy. The country was economically crippled, haemorrhaging in the wake of a spiralling brain drain and more famous for its export of Johnny Logan than the traditional spud. I think the words of Victor O'Reilly on his excellent website encapsulated 1980s Ireland best: 'A great place to visit or even to retire to but a terrible environment for business unless you were a publican, owned one of the larger farms or worked for the state (and almost everyone seemed to work for the state).'

Having moved to the very pleasant neighbourhood of Watson Road in Johnstown, Killiney, when I was twelve, it made perfect sense that my parents would send me to a local secondary school, preferably one that could be reached comfortably enough by bike or foot. My best mate Dave Burke lived just ten doors down and another footballing mate, Dave Forkin, ten doors further down again. I first met Dave Burke properly at his brother Andrew's funeral some years previously. Andrew had died tragically just six months before his father. Dave was a really great mate, always cheerful and gifted at music, like his two older brothers Rob and Tony . His mum Etta would one day become my best friend in the whole world, though I hardly knew it at the time.

Clonkeen College in Deansgrange, which was a pleasant thirty-minute bike ride away, is where we were all sent. The saying goes that your schooldays are the best days of your life and, in my case, this cliché is more than true. Without exception, those were to become six of the very best years of mine.

The school began life interestingly, as St Joseph's Private Preparatory School in September 1965 before becoming a secondary school two years later. It operates, to my mind, on the very same principles as a family might: you get out what you put in. Each stakeholder is responsible for an equal input, be they teacher or pupil, but people would always be available to support you in times of crisis without prejudice or judgement.

It was a non-fee-paying school and despite the usual shortages in funding, the school in my time managed just fine when it came to providing equipment, jerseys or transport. Thinking back, I'm not sure what it was that impressed me most about the place. The fact that equal emphasis was placed on education and sport? The fact that there was always a welcoming atmosphere? Or maybe, it was important that every one of those teachers gave everything they had to ensure we came out as rounded individuals and worthy ambassadors.

One of the reasons the teachers worked so very well as a unit was because the core had all come together ten or so years earlier in the mid-to-late 1970s, when the school was finding its feet. When Dom Toomey, or 'Domo' as we affectionately knew him, joined the school in the mid-1970s (today, he's the vice-principal), the sixth years ran their own football team. Domo is a talented man and I will be eternally grateful for what he and so many others like him did for me in Clonkeen.

Domo wasn't the only skilful sporting gem in the pack mind you. Other teachers had also excelled. Billy Noonan our small cuddly Commerce teacher, better known to the pupils as 'Spolge', had made the Cork minor football panel. Brendan Toomey, our careers advisor, made the Dublin minor hurlers and his successor Eamonn O'Hora would go on to play soccer with the likes of Paul McGrath. Mick

Brennan, our PE teacher, had played with the Carlow minors and, just for good measure, our English and history scholar Jim Byrne fenced for UCD. I remember those skills coming in rather handy in helping to protect the students from a nasty occurrence when I was in third year after a bad skirmish with some locals following a school disco.

Despite a poor self-image and an acne-ridden face, I felt safe once I was within the school grounds from the very first day in September 1982. *Rocky III* was the big movie of the day and everyone was either listening to 'Eye of the Tiger' by Survivor or, if you were really cool, you were welcomed in by Madness' 'House of Fun'. I could run fast, kick a ball an incredible distance off the ground and loved badminton and so threw myself into just about every sporting activity going. I even made the chess team which was run by the then principal Brother Nolan.

A very brilliant teacher from my primary school, Mrs Brooks, had encouraged me to play chess and, though I could never beat her son, Frank, I found the game a welcome distraction that forced me to concentrate for long periods.

We just managed to avoid corporal punishment which had been done away with in 1981. One thing we couldn't seem to avoid, though, were the crummy haircuts we had to have. Every guy wanted cool, long hair that looked like substantially more than a mere rat's tail falling from his neckline! Then there were the loafers and Harrington SKA jackets that defined a bloke's stance on music – were you a mod or a ska head? Or did you secretly watch *Fame* and go around listening to Irene Cara on your Walkman with the sound turned low as you walked up and down the school corridors?

Despite my devotion to sport and all things extracurricular, I somehow managed to scrape by in the classroom much to the bewilderment of many of my teachers. John Keogh, who took me for Geography right through school, used to laugh when he'd see me coming into class in my dishevelled state, hair uncombed, unshaven and looking generally the worse for wear. When I met John very recently following the Seven Summits Challenge, the first thing he asked in amusement was how I hadn't got lost on Everest.

I loved languages and, in that regard, relished my classes with Jim Byrne (English and History), Domo (French) and the man who would eventually become the current principal of the school, Mr Neil 'Cool Hand Luke' O'Toole. I swear that man could have eaten more eggs under pressure than Paul Newman. Having decided to stay back and do fifth year again (missed the first one: I was never there as I was playing for all the different sports teams), I felt the wrath one particular morning of Cool Hand O'Toole when I upset him in one of his French classes. I was being a complete idiot as it happens and deserved the considerable tongue lashing I received outside. Staying back, probably made me think I was cooler than I was, playing to the gallery of lads that I had joined.

We enjoyed wonderful success in sport during my time there. Everyone used to love Domo's passionate, fiery speeches before Gaelic football games. We won more matches on the back of that inspiration than perhaps we had a right to, even reaching Croke Park in 1985 for the schools final of the U16 A Schools, where we scraped a draw against a much-fancied Moyle Park side. Domo made us realise from an early stage that understanding what it was to have self-belief was far more important than acquiring the belief in the first place. Under the guidance of the three wise men (Domo, Mick Brennan and Brother Kelly), Clonkeen College football, and sport in general, prospered throughout the 1980s. Ten years earlier, the school had made its initial breakthrough onto the Gaelic map by winning through from Division C up to Senior. Among those crusaders that furrowed the ground for us all to follow was a rather talented young footballer by the name of Tommy Lyons, an ex-pupil who would go on to make his mark in Dublin football many years later.

If it was guys like Jim Byrne, Domo, Neil and John Keogh who motivated me, it was Brother Kelly who truly inspired me. To this day, I owe that man the biggest debt of gratitude. Firstly, I would never have been offered a place in UCD were it not for a conversation that we had behind the bike sheds on a balmy sunny afternoon after Paper 1 in English on the first day of the Leaving Cert in 1988. Brother Kelly noticed I wasn't in the best of form coming out of the exam: 'Surely, man, you didn't have problems with that paper did you, Master McKeever?'

'No, Brother,' I said, head down around my ankles, 'but I might have serious problems passing Maths 1 in the morning.'

'Blazes Kate!' he piped up. 'What in God's name were you doing in Mrs Summer's class for the past two years?' The answer to that was very little, as I had spent more time outside the class than inside it. 'Right, man,' arms flapping in the air, 'follow me. Get your jotter and pen out. We're going to cover Paper 1 this afternoon!'

Sure enough, Brother Kelly demystified theorems, unscrambled trigonometry and, in the space of two hours, made me believe that I could actually pass the paper.

He did exactly the same thing for the second paper as well. I passed Pass Maths, a subject I was otherwise certain to fail abysmally. I was good at everything else, sitting all honours subjects, but Maths was my serious Achilles' heel that had held me up since I had left primary school.

Truth is, Brother Kelly was a walking, talking genius. He could and did teach everything in the school from Applied Maths to Biology, from Irish to Physics. But here's the thing. He made learning fun. Suddenly, photosynthesis would come to life and burn brightly in all our minds like the sunshine that used to fill the labs in which we were sitting so attentively for his Biology classes.

At one point, my father was going to take me out of the school and put me in Blackrock College. I had just missed the opportunity to do the new fourth year, or transition year, and some parents at the time, including my own, were concerned that perhaps three years was the correct course of preparation for the Leaving Cert. Brother Kelly was quick to intervene, thank God. He pointed out to my father in the nicest possible way that I had done precious little in my first spell in fifth year. My excuse lay in the fact that I had been playing on every sports team, and as Brother Kelly explained, I'd fly it second time round! Incredibly, ten of us ended up going down the same route; half the Gaelic team in fact led by a good mate of mine Larry O'Gara who would deservedly go on to become our sportsman of the year in Leaving Cert.

Apart from Brother Kelly, there was only one other Brother whom I recall from the monastery which was located right beside our school, a Brother Bradshaw, who really only taught religion in my day. A kindly soul and a great character himself. The story goes, that he won pints on the strength of his ability to catch flies in his hands. It's a skill he passed on with some success to the school's current principal Neil O'Toole, who still takes great pleasure in watching lads part with their money as they swipe their hand through the air trying to catch the fly.

Some of the friendships we form come early in life, from childhood days. Others come throughout the course of our schooldays and others even later still. It was a pure fluke that I happened to meet Lorraine McGovern through school. Her brothers Paul and Larry both went through Clonkeen, and Larry and I were in the same year throughout our days there. Without exception, Larry Mc was one of the easiest-going guys I have ever met. I had never been to their house but, one afternoon when we were in fifth year, Larry invited me around for lunch. Just before Larry got his keys out, the front door creaked open and this woman's face peered out. These striking big eyes were now focusing in my direction. 'Who are you?'

Before I could answer, she asked, 'Are you Larry's English teacher? Is he doing OK? I have had my concerns about Larry applying himself in school. He's bright but—'

Thankfully, Larry just managed to intervene, 'Mum, this is Ian. He's in my class.'

'Impossible, Larry. Look at this man. He looks so much older and speaks completely different to you!' Larry and I just turned to each other and began to laugh. I had truly found the Munster family – alive and well and residing in County Dublin and I'd just met Herman's wife Marilyn! Forget the pot of gold at the end of the rainbow, I thought, this was a far more interesting and worthwhile discovery!

When Laura was finally assured that I was indeed in her son's class, struggling with many of the same things that he was, she smiled and relaxed and we had a wonderful afternoon. The McGovern's would become like family to me. Over the years, they would discover that I was even odder and nuttier than they were! Larry's crazy, adorable, mad sisters Lorraine and Jane were real gems and, though Lorraine and I kissed once, we knew that we were going to be lifelong friends.

&&&

Anna Jarvis of Philadelphia was the lady who began the campaign that brought about the official observance of Mothers' Day in the United States. Her mother had died, and Anna wanted all mothers to be remembered. She asked that white carnations be the official Mothers' Day symbol and, in 1914, President Woodrow Wilson signed the orders that made Mothers' Day a national holiday in America. I guess in a way the world was finally recognising that the role a mum plays in her child's life – boy or girl – is integral to the person they become.

Despite the fact that, even at the best of times, I made life difficult for my parents, particularly my mum, as a typically sulky and bolshy teenager, I owe a great deal in terms of the person I am today to my mum.

When I was much younger, I can vividly remember my mother's mother coming over to live with us. She died eventually after being with us for a number of years. She was a wonderful grandmother to both Denise and myself and we were very sad when she died. There's something very special about the bond that forms between a child and its grandparents.

Perhaps one of the reasons why I made life difficult for my mum was the fact that I didn't talk to her about being adopted. I closed up on the subject completely in my teenage years. My mum and I were very different as people too. She didn't believe in having meaningless conversations about the weather. It wasn't her style. She was a very direct and honest person and only said something that she felt was relevant. I guess, perhaps, I found her approach cold. But to be fair to her, she always spoke the truth and got straight to the point.

I'll always recall a conversation that we had after the Inter Cert results. Back then it was considered quite an achievement to secure nine honours in the Inter. (In fact, I have to say, that just like property prices, I think we've lost the plot when it comes to exam results. The overemphasis placed on exam results stinks: 'You only got an A2!')

A group of us decided we'd celebrate our efforts in true fashion. Dressed in those famous Talking Head suits, made so cool after the band's *Stop Making Sense* video, we marched ourselves up to Blinker's nightclub, beside the Leopardstown racecourse and the back of Foxrock Golf Club (the southside's answer to Tomangoes!). This was the place for under-eighteen-year-old lads to try their hand at looking older. We breezed it. It was an amazing experience and, as I was about to discover as I drank alcohol at a bar for the first time, everything that's a challenge in life is always perceived as being more rewarding. I also had my first kiss in a nightclub with a girl called Mairead. What a night! Everyone scored and the lads crawled home happy with five or six golf balls in each pocket.

I rose with a smile on my face the next morning as you'd expect. At the breakfast table, my sister was looking at me as if I'd just acquired the crown jewels. 'Hey, Mum, what a gorgeous day, eh?' Mum just went about her business getting ready for work: 'You arrived in here after 4 a.m. I presume you look like the cat that drank the cream because you got lucky with some poor unsuspecting girl?' As I mentioned, Mum didn't do small talk. I was fifteen going on fifteen at the time. A kiss was about as far as I had been. Mairead from Blinker's was only the second girl I had ever kissed. Mum was giving me way too much credit, though I suspect she didn't mean to really credit me at the time.

The one and only thought that was going through my head at the particular moment was whether Mum and me would one day have a drink together and just have a laugh as mates. That day would come.

3

What's in a Kiss?

'That love is all there is, is all we know of love.'
Emily Dickinson

What is about our first love that can make us blush and suddenly become all childlike in fellow adult company? Perhaps it's that first love is a little foolishness and a lot of curiosity, as George Bernard Shaw so eloquently put it, or maybe it's the fact that the magic of first love is our blissful ignorance that it can never end, as Benjamin Disraeli thoughtfully observed in between parliamentary sessions.

Undoubtedly for a young lad growing up, self-confidence breeds a more adventurous spirit, especially where the opposite sex is concerned. I remember when I was about thirteen, and at least a year from my first real kiss, a certain ritual that used to take place beside our local church, Our Lady of Good Council, in Johnstown. There was a vibrant youth-club scene at the time which kept us all amused and, for the most part, out of trouble. The youth club operated in a small building beside the actual church and, apart from anything else, fuelled my early love of cinema and the movies. My first real memory of watching movies was in that very same hall area. Roger Moore had just played Bond again in *Octopussy* and every young lad was in love with Maud Adams. The hall was also used by my local soccer team, Cabinteely Boys Football Club, and was where we had our end-of-year presentations, with proud parents looking on. The club also gave me an opportunity to meet girls.

Every night after the youth club finished, the lads and the girls walked across the grass and gathered ceremoniously under the street lamp across the way. Everybody used to huddle together like flies around a lamp waiting for the first couple to make their move and then somebody was charged with timing the duration of the ensuing 'Frenchie'. Bragging rights were reserved for those guys who could manage to keep the girl interested enough to kiss for longer than two minutes. I believe the record stood at just under four minutes. I used to stand enviously watching others, wondering if my turn would ever come. It turned out, probably by the simple laws of rotation, that I was eventually to ask a girl called Yvonne to kiss. I managed to pluck up the courage to ask her to meet me on one of the evenings after the youth club, but then, when it came to the crunch, I made my excuses to the lads and promptly left before any further embarrassment could ensue.

Back in those days, if my parents went away, my sister Denise was sent to stay with cousins and I was fortunate enough to be sent to 'Uncle Dermot's'. Technically, he was my father's cousin but, for all intents and purposes, was more like an uncle to me. Dermot was quite a character in every sense of the word. He'd become a priest following a series of bizarre incidents during the Second World War when he was posted as an engineer in Malaysia. Twice, the boat he was travelling on was bombed by the Japanese, and twice he survived. Taking this to be an act of God, Dermot decided to repay the man in the sky with a life in the priesthood. He had served as chaplain in the University of Bath, and as the parish priest in Rathnew in Wicklow. By the time our paths began to cross, he had, in effect, retired and happily just served mass to the St Raphael nuns in Stillorgan. He lived in a cool apartment in Sandycove, quite near where the old Forum Cinema used to be.

The man had incredible stories and wisdom to impart. I have never met anyone who could tell a better joke in my entire life. Most mornings would begin with Dermot singing some witty, but dirty, Limerick or other. I told my mate Dave on many occasions that he simply had to come and do a stay over. So one night, he did. Dermot ditched his collar and the three of us hit Dún Laoghaire, starting in

Scott's on the main street before falling into Stubbs's half-scuttered. We were two sixteen year olds having the time of their lives. I'm not sure Dave had ever got chatted up more in his entire life as Dermot kept the pub amused with fascinating war tales and funny jokes.

The nights out were a great relief, as things on the home front had hit a real low. Looking back, I was a complete pain to live with, moody and unforgiving to put it mildly. I was cracking up inside but not sharing with my family what I needed to get out. I was still harbouring insecurities that stemmed back to a misplaced sense of self-image and esteem. Why was the news of my adoption affecting me so badly?

I remember storming out of the house and running away to anyone who'd listen to me. I usually ended up in Dave's, being consoled by his mum Etta, at my pals the McGoverns or else at Paula's. I had met Paula, who was a gorgeous girl, and I told her that I was going to leave home, thinking it would be best for all concerned, and so I did. I moved into a flat in Dún Laoghaire, sharing with a guy who told me he was involved on the periphery with an amazing and gifted Wexford band called Cry Before Dawn. Looking back, I think he imagined it!

My diet went to pot and, within weeks, my skin, which had responded so well to antibiotics became worse than ever. I lost weight and struggled to do enough shifts in the local Horse & Hound pub to pay the rent and stay awake in school. There is no blame at all attached to my leaving home at seventeen. I simply had to do it or else I would have driven both my parents insane. Besides, I needed to get a taste of what it was like to live in the real world in the hope that I might eventually cop myself on.

By the time Paula and I split up a year later, it would be fair to say that I was mildly depressed. She didn't end it; I simply failed to turn up one Sunday afternoon. It was the day when the gang were meeting in Dalkey for drinks, and the same day that Pat Cash beat Ivan Lendl to capture the Wimbledon title. My self-confidence was at an all-time low and I had spent that particular afternoon lying out in the sun without any protection desperately trying to burn off the spots on my face. I couldn't even meet the one person who had been there through everything.

The fact that, two weeks earlier, I had come home to find the gardaí waiting for me at the flat hadn't helped matters. There was a headline in one of the national papers that read: 'Man Steals Mother's Rings'. Jewellery had also gone missing from other people's homes in the area and the guards wanted to interview me about the guy I would now no longer be living with. To be fair to my parents, they made a really huge effort when I moved back and life passed without much incident for the next year and a half.

In fact, it has to be said that, when I wasn't being a bolshy teenager, but was being respectful to my parents, life in the house was actually quite pleasant.

I was working with a recruitment agency in London, by the time the Leaving Cert results came out.

I had gone over earlier that summer with my cousin Mark, excited at the prospect of working in my first real job. I always remember getting my first CV done with little or nothing to put on it. My Inter results and lots of 'not a bad fella' testimonials, about summed it up. One of our other cousins, Charlie, who was several years older than us, was managing a really cool bar called Dizzie's in the Fleet Street area. Both he and his wife Stephanie helped us to land on our feet. Despite every attempt to convince myself otherwise, I knew I wasn't a brickie. In fact, despite the labourer shortages, I wouldn't have known one end of a brick from the other, and so it had to be office work for me. Working in the recruitment agency made me realise from a very early stage how much I enjoyed working with people.

I got to screen people in their first-phase applications for various engineering posts. In other words, I got to do the donkey work, but I loved it. I must have been there about a month when Dad rang me one evening in the house we were staying in – a very posh, four-bed detached in Fulham. England was going through the kind of madness we've been experiencing recently, where house prices are concerned, only this was the end of the 1980s and even garages were going for up to £75,000! Boarding the Dart in Dublin today reminds me of hopping on the Tube on the way to work each morning; sombre-faced individuals, expressionless, lost in their newspapers and devoid of chat.

Dad had phoned with the Leaving results. 'Do you want me to open them, so?' he asked. 'Just wait till I get my glasses so I can see the bloody things!'

No doubt I'll be found out now for that stunt! I thought. That stunt involved not sitting two of my exams for the actual Leaving Cert – Geography (not sure my geography teacher, knows this…) and Home Economics. We were all given the opportunity in sixth year to take Home Ec, if you did either Business Organisation or, as in my case, Biology. I knew that I could combine back then with the famous matriculation to get into UCD. Seeing as Trinity were offering a nasty matric that included the likes of Arabic, etc., I opted for the handier option of trying to get into UCD by sitting a supposedly 'common' paper that sat somewhere between honours and pass in terms of difficulty. You couldn't study for such a paper, but were expected to be able to sit it nevertheless, based on what you already knew and had covered. Boy was I in for a shock. Sitting throughout the entire Leaving and Matric, I had suffered terribly with hay fever as anyone who had the misfortune of sitting those same papers as me can testify. I also regularly had to borrow markers, pens in fact just about everything. I'll always remember one of my mates at the time looking exasperated after we'd sat the Biology paper, threatening to kill me if he didn't score at least a B, given all the interference he'd suffered from me sneezing down his neck.

By the time Dad and I had totted up the results, worked out down the phone, the three for a C and two for a D, and four for a B regime, we were starting to feel like contestants in *Sale of the Century*, waiting to see what we could afford behind the curtain. Despite failing English in the Matric (they couldn't read my appalling writing), two no sits and a host of other bizarre results, I was offered, among other things, Social Science. *The fun version of science?* I wondered, optimistically and rather naively. 'Let's go for it!' said Dad. To her credit, and despite the fact that I arrived a month late into the course, Dr Helen Burke had a place saved for me in the front of the class (sociology was taken in smaller rooms, classroom style) and so there was no place for me to hide, unlike in the big amphitheatre where I took Politics and Psychology.

The most amazing thing for me initially was to come to terms with the number of women on the course. Out of a class of ninety-odd, there were only five or six lads and we were thrust into a world of women as we sat timidly among the Amazonians of Sociology.

The one thing that I took away from my time in UCD, apart from a whole lot more self-confidence, was an inspiring theory from Sociology, the notion of relative depravation. The real meaning attached would one day help to save my life when I would find myself in a real life-and-death situation while stranded 8,200 metres above the ground.

The theory related to the depravation felt by the baby-faced US Marines relative to that of the hardened Japanese, whom they would face in horrendous hand-to-hand combat and literal fire fighting in the tunnels of the various islands like Iowa Jima that the Japanese had invaded. So in other words, no matter how bad you might think things are, there's always someone worse off. As I would discover later in life, it's important to maintain a sense of perspective.

By the time I turned twenty, I had decided to go to Australia. I was actually going out to see a girl that I'd met briefly called Annette. I was under strict instructions not to mess this up as her mum and dad were very close, long-standing friends of my parents. They used to come over to visit every so often. Annette and I were the same age and got on very well over the years as mates. In order to save the money to make that momentous journey back in 1990, I had taken a job in a well-known shop near the Loughlinstown roundabout heading southbound on the N11.

It would be one of the most memorable summers of my entire life. As it just so happened a few of the people working in the shop were gay. So what, I hear you ask? It's when you consider that we, shamefully, didn't decriminalise homosexuality for another three years that you come to appreciate that the whole gay scene was somewhat clandestine and remained underground at the time. Nobody wanted anyone who wasn't on the scene to know it existed.

These guys were wonderful and I had such great craic working with them. One night, the lads brought me on the absolute tear with them into the palpable heart of the gay scene in our capital city. We visited the Shaft, which used to be on Ely Place and I was brought to the infamous Hooray Henry's, which used to be located in the Powerscourt Centre. A guy asked me out to dance. Shocked, I began laughing nervously, to which he replied in complete indignation, 'How would you fancy it if a girl laughed in your face!' He had valid point. At that moment, he turned his head poised himself and gracefully marched off onto the dance floor to join the boys for their big anthem of the day, 'Vogue' by Madonna. Wow, could these lads dance! As someone who normally never got up without copious amount of alcohol, I certainly wasn't prepared to embarrass myself among this bunch of Astaires and Travoltas.

Later that evening, I was delighted and relieved to see a couple of the guys I'd been in school with. I shouted over, 'Hey lads what's the craic?' I've never seen a bunch of lads dive for cover so quickly. I guess, thinking about it, that it was really tough for them, and while I couldn't have cared less about a person's skin colour or sexual preference, they didn't know that.

Who can ever forget that famous summer, eh?

Italia '90. There was Roger Milla, the colourful Cameroonian that nearly broke English hearts and, of course, Schillaci, the Italian who would eventually break ours.

That particular summer we had an appropriately named Cocker Spaniel, Kinky. As kids growing up, we'd always had the company of dogs. Dad used to talk so fondly of Teddy, the dog he had as a kid and the tricks he used to teach him. One day, I brought Kinky in for his usual hair cut, important for dogs like Cockers to avoid canker in the ears, something I guess all long-haired dogs are pretty prone to. Dad had been warned expressly to wait thirty days following the dog's recent operation before taking him in. And so it was that, on that thirtieth day, Bonner famously saved and O'Leary thankfully scored, and our dog had a heart attack amid all the excitement and died on the operating table in the vet's and grooming clinic next door. I'll never forget Rhoda, the vet nurse, coming into the shop to tell me. Tears were running down my face, tears of joy at Ireland's epic victory over the Romanians and tears of genuine sadness at the news of my best pal dying at the ripe old age of fifteen.

Rhoda was a really kind-natured person and consoled me greatly that afternoon. She spoke openly about losing her brother tragically some years earlier and even offered to help us bury our dog on some land owned by her brother in Wicklow. I'll always recall very vividly driving down that evening to that hill in Enniskerry to say goodbye to our dog, staring blankly out the window as car horns were honked and people did beach-boy surfing impressions on top of cars. I had never seen our country unite in such a manner before. Ireland's success on the football pitch had come at such an important time for us all.

We'd all had enough of the bad times in the 1980s and now football had become a symbol of hope for all – Catholics and Protestants, guys and girls, gays and straights, it finally mattered not.

The months seemed to fly by and, before I knew it, I was preparing to go to Australia. Denise had been adamant that we replace Kinky for another less temperamental and frisky cocker. So we got Max, a cute and cuddly black one that was born, I reckon, without the capacity to growl. Just as well too, as I was always afraid a belated lawsuit might hit my parents for something his predecessor might have done. Max was named after Mel Gibson's Mad Max, whose posters still adorned my sister's bedroom. Denise wanted me to go on a fact-finding mission about Mr Gibson whilst in Australia, visit his ranch, arrange autographs – the usual sort of stuff associated, I guess, with a teenager and her first crush.

Max went in for his first groom two weeks before I was due to leave, around mid-December. Rhoda refused to take any money for the cut, saying it was the least she could do, with me going away. I was flattered and offered to buy her a drink to say thank you. I didn't drive at the time and have no idea how I managed to get to Wicklow that night to meet her in the Delgany Arms. What I do remember, though, is pretty comical. First, the question, which was facilitated by Dutch courage, 'Hey, Rhoda, how come you didn't speak to me until the dog died?' And the answer, 'That's cause I liked ya, Ian.' Then, the drunken payphone call to my father to announce that I wasn't coming home that night, despite the fact that I hadn't asked Rhoda if I could actually stay.

The night was topped off when, back at Rhoda's place and already drunk, we sat drinking vodka and cranberries till the early hours.

The next day we were snowed in. Rhoda's small but charming gate lodge, deep in the heart of County Wicklow had been transported onto a Hollywood-like winter wonderland set. When was the last time that happened in Ireland? Looking back, it was such a good thing, for although nothing had happened between us at that point, it gave us a chance to really get to know each other.

Four days later, when the snow finally melted, I'd been invited to join Rhoda at one of the vet's Christmas parties taking place in Dundrum. I'll never forget the conversation between myself and the very charming host of the party, Malcolm. 'Hey, Ian, when you and Rhoda walked in here together, there was such a chemistry between you guys, the whole room noticed it. You both have the 'Readybrek glow' thing going on. Life's short my friend. Never lack the courage to do what you believe is the right thing ...'

Driving to the airport with Dad on St Stephen's Day, I decided to heed Malcolm's words. I told Dad the whole truth about Rhoda and that I wasn't going to stay in Australia, but rather try and make things work with her. I think he drove around the airport roundabout twice in complete shock.

True to my word, I apologised in person to Annette and came home. Despite my decision, causing untold rifts among family and certain friends, Rhoda and I went for it and I treasure the year or so we had together. Rhoda had children and, in the end, Shannon, her eldest, wanted to go home to his father in France. I didn't get to see

Rhoda before she left. There was a note left with Dave's mum Etta where I was living.

My relationship with Rhoda had a profound effect on my life. It was the first time I understood what being in love was all about. The consequences had been pretty severe for both of us, it has to be said. The biggest for me wasn't moving out of home but that I wasn't sure I'd ever really be able to open my heart up again.

4
Pastures New

'My best friend is the man who, in wishing me well,
wishes it for my sake.'

Aristotle

When was the last time any of us took just five minutes away from our precious mobile phones and busy lives to just simply stop and be? Many people that do decide to reflect, find some comfort in the principles attached to yin and yang, the cornerstone of Taoism and traditional Chinese medicine. People come to accept that every action has a consequence and that every decision is a responsibility to shoulder. There is a belief that this concept offers insight about how opposite forces in our universe can, in fact, be complementary.

People often ask me why I became so involved with charity work and why I felt this constant need to try to change the world for the better. The answer in truth is simple – I believe one person can, and in fact should, make a real difference. The catalyst for my action? A movie, strange as that may seem, entitled *The Power of One* which starred Morgan Freeman. It changed my outlook on life forever when I first watched it in 1992.

The film tells the story of Peter Philip Kenneth Keith, or PK as he is affectionately known. PK is an English boy born in South Africa, who is bullied at the Afrikaner boarding school he has been sent to. During his time at school, his mother dies and PK is left as an orphan, so he is sent to his grandfather's German friend, Doc, who agrees to look after him. Doc takes PK out of the boarding school and educates him himself. The Second World War is raging and, eventually, Doc is forced into a prison camp until the war ends. PK goes with him and it is here that he meets his second mentor, Geel Pete (played by Morgan Freeman), who teaches PK the art of boxing and insists that PK is the 'rainmaker', the one who will bring freedom to the Africans, and end apartheid.

The film then shows an older PK, a year before he goes to university. He continues his boxing and meets his love Maria, who is the daughter of the Afrikaner Nationalist President, who disapproves of PK and his 'English attitude'. Against her father's will, Maria continues to see PK and helps him to start a school to teach South Africans how to read and write English. This creates untold problems with the Afrikaner police. PK is forced to choose and stands up for what he truly believes in, regardless of the consequences. As an impressionable twenty-two-year-old, similar in age to PK, I was already beginning to believe that to truly heal any person you must first raise their spirit, though I had little idea of how to help anyone at the time, least of all myself.

Not that I was doing too much for charity in 1992. I was now studying by night for the very popular two-year certificate in Public Relations in the Royal College of Surgeons. Once again, not unlike the degree course in Social Science, the course was heavily populated with women. In fact, of the 102 in my class, only eight of us were men.

I owe much to at least two of my male colleagues. Craig, a highly likeable guy, ignited my latent passion for the game of rugby. He was quite content to play on the wing for Lansdowne, no mean achievement back in the days before the Heineken Cup. I rapidly discovered two things about rugby from Craig. One, I could actually kick a rugby ball further off the ground than I could a Gaelic football. And, two, I was very fast from a standing start and so the wing became a position that fascinated me, offering the chance to fly like an express train and score glorious tries. Of course, there was just one small problem. I wasn't built like a rugby player. At the time, I wasn't doing weights or putting on the calories in any controlled sense. It became clear, after much soul searching that my love of rugby would have to therefore be confined to watching from the sidelines.

Martin is someone that I deeply admire. He was friends with both me and Craig throughout the course, and was the musically enlightened one among us. It was in his flat one night that I became a devoted fan of Lyle Lovett, the very gifted musician who sadly became better known in the 1990s for marrying Julia Roberts. I think it might have been on that same night that Martin told me that he was HIV positive. A blood transfusion had done the damage. From him, I learned a very important lesson which many years later would help to save my life – it's not the things that go wrong in our lives that matter, its how we chose to deal with them that really measures you.

I was working on Dublin's South William Street at the time, in a company called Avelbury Publishers, where, among other things, I learned how to sell advertising space and sell it well. Today, my own PR students look up at me in horror when I ask them on the first night to differentiate between advertising and public relations. Of course, the well informed will usually reply with the standard textbook answer: 'Advertising is about selling and PR is about telling.' Their faces normally turn white when I tell them that PR is all about selling and that, in fact, we are all selling something. They then become more worried when I go on to tell them that, to be truly successful in PR, they must learn to understand that it is only the commodity that differs – advertising space, insurance or the required column inches for the client in the newspapers, for example. It is really only then, in the response to the needs of the client that we see the value of the PR tools in play, complementing the role of the marketeer.

It's at this point that those who decide they are prepared to stick the course sit back and prepare themselves for what is ahead, whilst those who have already decided PR isn't for them plan a quick exit.

The certificate course, as it was when I studied it, certainly helped to change the way we sold in Avelbury. In fact, everything benefited as a direct result. The main focus in the company at the time was on materials for education and various yearbooks which were produced for ex-pats abroad or living out of their respective counties.

Those four very successful and informative years at Avelbury, from 1991 to 1994, taught me how to survive in the dog-eat-dog world of publishing and sales. The fact that I ended up being brought into St Michael's Hospital late in 1994 with a bleeding ulcer has no bearing on the job or the company. The fact that I smoked like a trooper and had a bad diet was the real reason I ended up in so much trouble.

I'll never forget one particular afternoon – two days before I was hospitalised – going over to Grogan's pub on South William Street for what had become my proverbial cheese sandwich and pint of milk. These two comforts were required so that I could continue to smoke without collapsing in sheer pain. I heard a very distinctive and pronounced voice across the bar, as the barman poured my milk, 'One should only put Guinness into that glass.' I remember wincing back in some discomfort at the rather familiar face of one of my favourite actors, the great Richard Harris. Needless to say, milk wasn't the only thing I drank that particular lunchtime, as I thoroughly enjoyed the company of one of the acting world's larger than life characters, quickly forgetting the physical pain I was in.

What is it about being in our twenties that makes us feel all-powerful and unstoppable? Perhaps it's our ability to recover quickly from the previous nights over-indulgence? What about our insatiable appetites? Believing we can eat as many pizzas, biscuits, chocolate bars and late-night kebabs as we chose because we have so much pent up nervous energy that we will burn the lot off in a matter of hours. Those of us who smoked did so without any hint of regret or remorse – our bodies as yet unwilling to reject that disgusting first drag, that grotty inhalation first thing in the morning.

I was your classic candle-burner. Although I think I worked extremely hard throughout my twenties, I partied most nights like my life depended on it. I've lost count of the number of mornings I came directly from Leeson Street's club scene virtually straight into work.

Dr Gary Brow, the hospital consultant to Loughlinstown, correctly observed that if I didn't quit smoking, the hospital simply wouldn't treat me again. Although I actually didn't quit in the immediate aftermath of being hospitalised, I did make some changes. I started to drink Guinness instead of lager. Although the bitter taste took some getting used to, it nevertheless helped my stomach considerably. I also left Avelbury Publishing.

There is only so much time anyone can spend in the pressure cooker before they, inevitably, explode. Not unlike the athlete who doesn't know when to stop and listen to their body and ends up overtraining, there comes a point when you are forced to look at things in a different light. My time at Avelbury had been well spent, but it was time to move on and explore new environments.

A great pal of mine and, in essence, my mentor John T. Murphy took me aside after I had recovered and started to help me consider what it was that I actually wanted out of life. John was encouraging me to finish the required elements to my President's Gold Award.

To earn a Gold Award, you have to achieve certain personal goals over a two-year period under the guidance of a PAL (award leader) in four distinct areas: personal development, community involvement, sport and outdoor activity. Apart from the level of difficulty, which would naturally increase with time, the key distinction between earning a Bronze Award, for example, and a Gold Award was the time commitment; six months for bronze; a year for silver and two years for gold.

He also wanted someone to help the *Gaisce* office to produce a tenth-anniversary publication – *Gaisce: Ten Years in Ireland* – and to deal with the various other PR bits and pieces that would be arising to mark the tenth anniversary of the awards in 1995, not least the planned visit of Prince Edward at the end of that year. In truth, I was delighted to take John up on his kind offer and the CEO at the time, another John Murphy, happily supported my twelve-month secondment.

I attacked the project in January 1995 with total commitment and passion. The corporate world responded magnificently to the publication in terms of financial support. There was a genuine sense of recognition for the important role that the awards played in the lives of Irish people under the age of twenty-five. Six months later, Gay Byrne was happy to do the honours at the book launch.

Things were going reasonably well for me at that point. I was living with Marguerite, who was also my best friend in the world. I had also finally learned to drive and got my first car, a battered old Mazda 323. I'll never forget taking my first spin into town that year with Marguerite's mum, Theresa, as my co-pilot. Coming onto Pearse Street, I thought I was going to kill us both! Needless to say, I didn't pass the test the first time. In fact, in Walkinstown, I completely ignored the instructor's command to take the second exit off the roundabout and instead went twice around one of the most dangerous roundabouts in the entire country. But inevitably, as I began to clock up the miles in my old Mazda, and given that bond that develops between man and his first machine, so my confidence eventually grew and my driving improved. I got my test second time round, passed it in fact with flying colours, despite having to avoid a flying dustbin in the streets of Ranelagh.

As preparations began to take formal shape for the arrival of Prince Edward, we had a shortlist of twenty-five recipients who would be presented officially with their gold medals by President Mary Robinson. There was just one problem, as John T. reminded me one morning, 'You deserve to be taking your place in with the rest of the crew. You just need to complete your venture activity. So finger out, Ian, and make it happen or you will regret it for the rest of your life!'

Venture activity? How was I going to plan one of those in hurry? I needed something meaningful, something that was well-planned, would last four days and benefit somebody or something.

That very same night, I was sitting in the bath and suddenly as I caught my reflection in the mirror, my nose extremely red from being out in the cold wind earlier, it just came to me! 'Eureka!' I exclaimed. I leapt out of the bath and ran downstairs to share my good news with a rather perplexed Marguerite. 'Why would you possibly want to do something as insane as that?' she asked.

'Because, it's different and will grab people's attention!' I belted out, beside myself with sheer excitement. I even had a name for this master plan, my deliverance from an otherwise sticky situation at the upcoming awards ceremony: Operation Rudolph.

I was going to dress in full Santa Claus regalia and cycle 200 miles in support of a deserving charity and I was going to do it in four days. I was also going to make sure the media bought into the whole shebang. Santa on his bike delivering presents to sick children in the run up to Christmas. It was perfect.

And so on 20 December 1995, the country's inaugural Santa cycle took place. Leaving from Our Lady's Hospital in Crumlin, I, in my Santa suit, headed south through Wicklow and eventually make my way to a massive party planned for the children at the regional hospital in Waterford. As Alan Betson from *The Irish Times,* one of the country's most gifted press photographers, weaved his magic with Santa and the kids at the off, I was filled with an amazing feeling of genuine optimism – that inexplicable feeling that says that what you are about to do is wholly significant, though you have absolutely no real comprehension of why at the time.

The charity I had decided to support was a wonderful project entitled the Bubble Gum Club, founded by Peter Harris, a very good pal of mine.

Peter had been quite successful in his own career, developing a profitable courier business among other things and so desperately wanted to give back. His dream was to help sick children who were beyond medical assistance – to put a genuine smile on their faces before they died. The principles were not unlike those of the Share a Dream/Make a Wish Foundation. Except that, in Peter's case, it would always be the intention to help groups of children rather than focusing on the specific needs of one child which the other charities did with tremendous dignity. As the Bubble Gum Club was in its infancy at that time, any help that I provided would make a genuine difference, not just in monetary terms but crucially in helping to raise awareness. I couldn't wait to see these children smiling.

I was in such a buoyant mood leaving Our Lady's Hospital that nothing and no one was going to rain on my parade. I'll never forget what happened as I got back on to my bike that afternoon in Camolin, County Wicklow. I had been cycling for about five hours by that stage and the weather had been remarkably kind to me. As I left the village, I noticed this old blue Ford Escort pulling up alongside, which I remembered cycling past about twenty miles previously. There were two middle-aged women from the northside of Dublin sitting inside and they were holding the front of the *Evening Herald* aloft. 'Oh my God, that's me!' I shouted, peering in at the paper. It was all I could do not to crash the bike.

'Hey, Santy,' one of the ladies shouted out, 'any chance of gettin' in here and giving Deirdre an early Christmas pressie?' As the women drove off in fits of laughter, I smiled thinking that at least the message was getting out there. The next couple of days passed with very little incident. Despite heavy rain on the third day, I was having the best time of my life and the public were terrific in their support. Every big truck that passed would honk its horn in an even more sustained and more inspiring fashion than the last one and cars would continually flash their lights. I linked up daily with the various local stations and press and RTÉ continued to give support on various 2fm shows, with Tony Fenton leading the updates.

As I sat waiting for my garda escort outside the final petrol station before I began the last kilometre into Waterford city, I decided to light myself a well-earned cigarette. 'Wouldn't want the children to see Santa smoking, now, would we?' The guard had arrived ahead of schedule! Embarrassed, I quickly stubbed out the fag and began the final triumphant free wheel into An Deise. It was a truly wonderful buzz and those special hours spent in the Regional with some of the nicest kids I've ever met was a genuine privilege in the truest sense of the word.

I guess I could hardly have known at the time that this mad but inspired idea born in the bath would become an annual feature of Christmas for the next ten years. During those years, literally hundreds of members of the public and media alike left their respectable worlds and disappeared across the roads of Ireland on bikes. People including Barbara Power and Annette O'Meara, with her infectious laugher, and Pascal Sheehy. Guys like Paul Collins, Mario Rosenstock and Wes Darcy, all of whom brought their own special brand of humour to the gig.

There were many friends and colleagues who gave their time voluntarily and willingly to do their bit for charity. A small core group of people made up the working group; they included two good friends from the Gaisce scene, Gordon Ward and Stephen Peers, and an old PR colleague Sinead Whooley. Each year, different charities were picked to receive the money raised. As the success grew, we were able to include more charities – Aware, the Alzheimer Society and the Marie Keating Foundation of Ireland were among some of the better known charities to benefit.

I'll always remember meeting the new CEO of the ISPCC Paul Gilligan in 1999 and being able to bring the ISPCC on board at a time when the charity was receiving so much unfortunate press for alleged financial wrongdoings by the organisation's former chief executive. In total, Operation Rudolph helped over twenty different causes to varying degrees and raised hundreds of thousands of pounds and euros in the process. Quite apart from the cycles, other things were done to raise funds. Much credit is due here to Pfizer Ireland for helping the committee find its feet with support and sponsorship.

In 2001, for example, together with the support of Maeve Butler and thousands of kids involved with Faroige up and down the country, we set about creating the world's largest coin mural to mark the official changeover to the euro. We gathered 1.6 million coins from across the country through the Ulster Bank branch network. Irish Rail's fast track division were incredible, moving money from A to B as a matter of priority and without any charge. The incredible mural – which was designed by one of the committee at the time, the designer Hugh Trayor – was to be placed by kind permission at the front of the Collins Barrack's. Hugh had suggested together with the experts in the museum that we recreate the shape of the first coin minted in Ireland in 995 AD. The finished work, which saw hundreds of children filling in the actual mural design with coins, was visually stunning and the Air Corps facilitated the media by flying them 200 feet above the mural to photograph it.

Several years earlier, when working in AA Roadwatch, Lorraine Keane had introduced me to a pal of hers, Willow Ward whose mum had died tragically of cancer, hoping that I might be able to help Willow achieve her ambition. What followed was not only a wonderful friendship but the opportunity to help someone for the first time in a truly meaningful way. Together we would get to work on two of the best and most rewarding fundraisers that two people could have achieved.

It was Willow's intention that a book of well-known recipes be complied to raise for funds for St Luke's Hospital. The first time I met Willow, she had a folder with her and a collection of maybe twenty typed recipes. We worked together for several years as friends on this and one other project. To Willow's credit, her first compilation entitled *Food For Thought* went to number three in the bestseller list.

Our next voluntary assignment was to help a fledgling organisation which had been set up by Ronan Keating and his sister Linda, in memory of their mum Marie who had also died of cancer. It struck me that Willow should do another book to help, and so the idea for *Anything But Balls* – in which various footballers gave ten facts about themselves – was born. Players from across the world donated their shared memories and Amstel lager (Champion's League sponsors at the time) became the book's sponsor. There were two-mile queues down O'Connell Street as we invited Ronan, George Best and Brian Kennedy to join Willow for the special book signing in Eason's. Famously, George asked me to get a Chardonnay for the signings. When I returned with the bottle, he replied, 'No, Ian, I meant a case.' George was a pleasure to work with and it was only fitting that, on the night of the book launch and auction, he was presented with a stunning piece of Waterford crystal shaped in a globe inscribed with the words: 'To the greatest of them all. Thanks for the memories.' The man was a legend. The book, with a foreword by the singer George Michael, became a bestseller, and the initial funds of €125,000 required for the mobilisation of the cancer care units were successfully raised.

Of course, all that glitters is simply not gold and, by 2002, I soon found myself dealing with the sort of horrible situations that can occur when things go wrong. Operation Rudolph's motley crew of myself and a bunch of other unpaid volunteers, had many common goals. We were committed to the simple notion of making a difference, raising public awareness and helping deserving causes – in between the day jobs. This was set out in our memorandum and articles of association. Under good advice from the man who would later be appointed CEO of the Marie Keating Foundation, David Hall, Operation Rudolph finally became a limited company and sought charitable status. We were not the best at keeping records, receipts or proper paper trails up to that point, we were just a bunch of guys having fun doing our bit for charity.

I'd be the first to admit that I was by far the worst culprit. Were it not for Cian Browne, our multi-talented administrator at the time, and Sinead Whooley, we would never have completed the charitable status application properly. But we did, and that's what counts. I was lucky to have good people around me, it certainly compensated for my lack of ability to process the simple tasks in life. But, nevertheless, I was learning another valuable lesson, it's always the sum of our parts that make us truly strong.

5

Never a Liar, a Thief or a Smoker Be

'Only those who dare to fail greatly can ever achieve greatly.'
Robert Kennedy

After Lorraine Keane left AA Roadwatch in pursuit of pastures new over on TV3, the department was initially taken over for a while by Karen Chewe, the blonde who drove all the boys mad on Today FM with her husky tones. We had quite a crew in my time – Emma Caulfield, Trevor Keegan, Ruth Scott, Nuala Carey and Lisa Armstrong. It's incredible to think that each and every one of them has gone on to enjoy successful careers in related areas of the media, be it radio or television.

The circumstances in which I joined Roadwatch, mind you, were a little bizarre. Lorraine and Karen had decided to take up the night diploma in public relations that I was lecturing on at the time in the Royal College of Surgeons. One particular evening, the conversation (steered by me) converged on the subject of roundabouts. Those who listened to RTÉ Radio had a fascination with the way Lorraine pronounced the word 'roundabout'. Lorraine's accent was unaffected to my mind. She came from Templeogue and was as down to earth as any girl I'd ever met – so what was the big deal? I certainly didn't get it, hence my curiosity that evening. To her credit, Lorraine took the questions in her stride, seeming genuinely surprised that such a trivial thing was occupying the minds of the RTÉ audience. 'Hey, Ian,' she added, 'myself and Karen would love to hear your attempt at a traffic report. Only if you're up for it, of course!' A challenge! Laid down in front of the whole class. How could I resist?

In truth, I hadn't the faintest clue about to how to put a traffic report together. *How difficult can this really be?* I thought to myself. But what started out as a bit of a joke rapidly became a source of genuine embarrassment.

Right, Mc, pull yourself together and start writing! I didn't seem to be able to get past the thought of frustrated motorists all stuck on various routes. Which routes should take priority? How many different ways can you actually say the same thing? Heavy, voluminous, car park – help! And so I turned to my wordsmith, my buddy with the golden tongue who hailed from Thurles, Paul Hayes. Paul was never short of a word or two.

ಚಿಚಿಚಿ

The previous year, Paul and I had worked on a gig together on behalf of a client of mine – the Break for the Border group. After finishing my very successful and rewarding year with the guys in Gaisce, I had decided to strike out in the big bad world of PR with a pal of mine, Laura. We were young and determined to change the world in which we worked. We brought a certain passion and genuine desire to want to explore things and tried to always have a fresh perspective! Not surprisingly, given our love for all things charity, we worked on a great many projects that held a connection to helping to improve the lives of others.

Tony Leach practically ran the Break for Border group. He seemed to be everywhere and appeared in each of the various pubs whenever he wanted, like the tailor in the Mr Benn cartoon. One afternoon, Tony turned to me and Paul in genuine frustration. 'I'm sick of these buckets!' he exclaimed. He was referring to the blue buckets that make an appearance every couple of years from the people who run the People in Need Appeal on RTÉ. Once again, Tony had been asked to place the buckets strategically around Café En Seine. 'Come on

McKeever, there must be some way we can show a little bit of imagination here and do something different with these flaming buckets, other than asking people to put money in them.' Drawing nervously on my Marlboro cigarette, I sat pensively for a moment. 'Leave it with me, mate,' was about all I could manage. I'm not sure Tony or anyone else in the group was quite expecting what followed in 1996.

In short, we held the Insane Café En Seine Dáil Duck Race – a race of 175 ducks on the River Liffey. Kathleen Lynch managed to round up a few of her Dáil colleagues to announce the madness by way of a photocall outside Café En Seine. Dressed in full duck costumes, they sipped blue cocktails which had been specially prepared by the bar staff inside. We had a hoot and the TDs were absolutely brilliant. Peter Thursfield from *The Irish Times* got a great shot of Kathleen dancing on one leg with a passing pedestrian. And so all the Break for the Border outlets were geared up for the big race in the Liffey. Paddy Power bookmakers took bets from the public as to which TD's duck might get over the proverbial line first and Jim Sherwin would adjudicate this very special race with the 175 blue ducks on the River Liffey. All of the media to be fair were tremendously supportive. We had suggested that the lads send in a blue duck to the weather people in RTÉ. Not to be outdone and to her credit Evelyn Cusack used our blue duck to herald that evening's weather announcement for the big race. Paul Hayes' caption which he had written up for the press release announcing the gig read: 'From the sublime to the reduckulous.'

🐤🐤🐤

Paul and I recorded the demo for AA Roadwatch on a tape recorder in his bedroom flat. Short of inspiration that particular afternoon, the most we could come with was a lorry load of chickens which had shed its load on the N7! Perhaps Lorraine took pity or perhaps she just admired me for rising to the challenge. I was amazed when they offered me the job. Denis Fisk who oversaw the Roadwatch Department had no problem with me working on a permanent but part-time basis so that I could keep my PR business running. So long, of course, as I was prepared to support any PR requirements the department might have from time to time. This brought me into contact with the man who acted as the official spokesperson for Roadwatch, Conor Faughan. If Paul Hayes was a wordsmith, then this man was a walking thesaurus! Apart from Dave Fanning or perhaps Rick O'Shea on 2fm, I've simply never heard anyone manage to say so much without drawing breath. Conor was, at the time, and still is today, the consummate professional who represented not only his organisation brilliantly but stood up for the rights of motorists magnificently. There simply is no better proactive PR professional anywhere in this country. I'm sure any of you who drives a car will somewhere down the line be very glad for this man's intervention on a whole range of issues from car taxes to road safety. Hardly surprising, then, that so many consultancies have tried to prise him away over the years.

During the time I worked with Roadwatch (1996–2000), the traffic reports on Today FM were sponsored by what was then eircell (now Vodafone) in a deal agreed with the then CEO Stephen Brewer. In reality, however, my own humble reports could have been sponsored by Kleenex given that most of them were written up in a hurry in the downstairs toilet on tissue paper! You're possibly starting to get the picture by now – the scruffy unshaven candle burner, who could have passed for Walter Mitty first thing in the morning!

I guess, in truth, I enjoy scrubbing up as much as the next man, but if I don't need to, I'm happy to chill out in a pair of combats and this is what happened in Roadwatch. It used to frighten me when I realised that people actually listened to our traffic reports. I assumed most people knew it was simply 'heavy' out there and would channel hop when the reports came on. But, as I quickly discovered, although most of what's contained in the actual sixty-second report is common sense (everyone knows where the traffic is heavy, let's face it), there are other nuggets of information that can be useful. Accidents, black spots, protest marches, sporting fixtures, etc. Perhaps if I'd attempted to make more of these opportunities, my reports might have held some nugget of useful information but, inevitably, more often than not they would skewer off in some random direction. Looking back, it's hardly surprising given the fun atmosphere we were working in.

I was really lucky to be linking in those days with some of the great presenters of our time. There was 'Iano' (Ian Dempsey) in the mornings, who had joined Today FM following a very long and successful career on 2FM. Ian had guys working with him at the time like the brilliant Mario Rosenstock, whose Gift Grub sketches have gone on to become the stuff of legend, and Undertones lead singer Paul McLoone who produced Ian's show back in those days. Even though I was the male voice complementing that of Karen's, Ian always made me feel exceptionally welcome on the show and we used to have real fun and craic on air. I think Ian's ability to not take himself too seriously and his uncanny knack of being able to relate to just about everyone make him one of the outstanding broadcasters of his generation.

People always recall Ian's time with the puppets Zig and Zag. One of my favourite on-air stories relates to an incident that occurred back in his 2fm days. Thanks to their sponsor Kellogg's, the guys were away somewhere in the US. Ian asked Zig (I think) where Zag was, to which the puppet replied, 'Out there sunning himself, Ian.' Eventually, Zag waltzed into the studio as Ian is mid-flight reminding listeners that they are in the States with thanks to Kellogg's when Zig piped up on air, 'Wow, Ian, look at Zag, he's as brown as a Weetabix!'

In the afternoon, I would have the pleasure of working with Phil Cawley and we remain good mates. Following Phil, arguably the man I had the most fun with on air was Eamon Dunphy. His show The Last Word remains to this day one of the best things to ever happen to Irish radio. Maybe one of the reasons that I liked him so much was the fact that he wasn't orthodox in what he did or said. I could wholly relate to that as I wasn't exactly that way inclined myself, let's face it! Eamon cared little for the traffic reports per se, but had a genuine curiosity to discover the person behind the links. It was as if anyone contributing to the programme had a personality that was worth bringing out from time to time. I was never one of those, to be fair, who took much of an interest in the whole 'Big Jack' v. Dunphy saga that peppered

Ireland's success on the football field in the late 1980s and early 1990s. Like most of us, I was simply caught up in the whole euphoria of beating England in Stuttgart and qualifying for the quarter-finals of the World Cup in Italia '90. One thing I do recall, however, very vividly in fact, was Eamon's 'hold it right there, Bill' comment. Who can forget the accompanying magic white pencil which guided us effortlessly across the screen as we watched in awe at the guttural powers of one Frank Rykard as he spat at his German opponent, in a match involving Germany and Holland. A game which the Dutch subsequently lost but will always be remembered for Eamon's amazing powers of visual perception!

I certainly enjoyed reading Eamon's column in the *Sunday Independent,* where, for the most part, I felt he was always prepared to put it on line and in the process often captured the mood of the nation. It was quite a thrill then to find myself linking with a man reborn on *The Last Word* programme in the evenings through AA Roadwatch.

ধ্যেখ্য

Like most people, I envisaged being married to someone as a commitment that you make for life. I first met Marguerite through a mutual friend of ours, who had studied law with her. They were both working part time in the Powerscourt Centre in Dublin when our paths first crossed.

I had rather stupidly broken up with a girl in college called Grainne Walshe, allowing my own insecurities to ruin a good thing. Even four years later when I met Marguerite, I still harboured feelings for Grainne. Grainne was, and still is, a gorgeous red head, who grew up in one of the very coolest houses I'd even seen or been in, but was modest and unaffected by money thanks to a very considered upbringing by her parents, Louis and Imelda. Grainne, however, was now seeing someone else – a great guy called Isaac whom she would go on to marry and have two wonderful children with.

It was the summer of 1993 and I'd just finished my PR certificate and had decided to stay very involved with both PR and the Public Relations Institute. For five years, I threw myself into the profession of public relations, keen to learn as much as I could. I had a particular interest in the educational side of things and especially the running of the certificate course which would go on to become a diploma, which complemented the existing post-graduate Masters option offered by DIT on Aungier Street. I fulfilled various roles on behalf of the PRI in running the course, including that of student liaison officer, exploring novel ways in which we could offer the students practical opportunities to apply the theories that they learned in class. One particular year, we forged links with Dr Mary Redmond and the Irish Hospice Foundation and the students developed a PR and fundraising programme to raise money and awareness for the hospice's excellent work.

Among the many things that were introduced was the idea of the breakfast club, at which various people came to speak to the students. Among the many who came to speak was Bertie Ahern, who was the Minister for Finance at the time.

Despite having a law qualification, Marguerite took up the PR diploma as well. The girl had brains to burn and was extremely modest about her talents. We hit it off from the start and, at the core of our relationship, were always the very best of friends. We got married at Christmas 1997. It was a gorgeous wedding that took place in Wooden Bridge as Marguerite came from Kiloughter outside Ashford. Though the marriage didn't last very long, out friendship endures to this day.

As I look back now, I wasn't ready perhaps to settle down – primarily because I wasn't settled in myself. I had never really taken the time to get to know myself properly and deal with certain things inside of myself.

6

If at First You Don't Succeed...

'The greatest inspiration is often born out of desperation.'
Comer Cottrell

The county of Wicklow, the Garden of Ireland, is renowned worldwide for its scenic beauty, and offers a variety of walking challenges, from woodlands and rolling hills to wild craggy mountain climbs. It is, to my mind, God's own back garden, the place he probably sat back and enjoyed a beer in after those initial six days of world creation!

The Wicklow Mountains lie just south of Dublin, of course. This, believe it or not, is the largest unbroken block of high-raised ground in Ireland, covering almost the same area as that of Mont Blanc in France, being almost fifty kilometres long and forty kilometres wide. Where the mountains meet the sea, some amazing paths run through sandy and stony beaches or up cliffs and hills, overlooking the whole of Dublin. It's simply an amazing way to let your soul run free.

As you turn off the N11 heading southbound at Kilmacanogue, you will see the sign for Wicklow's most frequented of sacred spots, Glendalough. There are, in fact, nine marked walking trails around this incredible 'Glen of the Two Lakes', ranging from the so-called 'easy' three-kilometre Green Road walk, to the 'hillwalking' eleven-kilometre (490-metre climb) and the famous Wicklow Way route. The Green Road is a wooded path along the Lower Lake from the ruins of the sixth-century monastic city to the great Upper Lake. Perhaps the loveliest walk of all, though, is the second toughest, the classic nine-kilometre (389-metre climb) Spinc and Glenealo Valley route – up along the rim of Glendalough Valley, overlooking the Upper Lake and dropping into Glenealo Valley to return by the Miners' Road to the Visitors' Centre, where a map showing these trails is available.

Today, I am certainly impressed with these hills, but I didn't always feel this way about the greatest outdoor gym in the country.

'Hey, Ian, call for you on line one. Some guy called John Morrison. Wants to talk to you about some climbing challenge or other.' Emma Caulfield was rushing into the AA Roadwatch studio as she spoke. We'd had a bad morning filled with serious accidents. There had even been a fatality in Limerick, or 'very serious accident' as we usually referred to them on air. To compound matters, I had just been clamped, again! The *Sunday Independent's* Gail Killilea had already run an article about the irony of the Roadwatch guy who had been clamped more times than anyone in the country (the count was at twenty-nine at that stage). Just how all that nonsense began on my part I'm really not sure. Carelessness? Hardly… Suffice to say, mountain challenges were the last thing on my mind. I knew nothing about mountains; besides why did he want to talk to me?

'So let me get this straight,' I said to John, 'you want to climb each of the mountains in Ireland and Britain in the fastest time possible by land and sea and you'd like Roadwatch to help out how exactly?' He explained that any publicity we could offer the challenge during the traffic reports would be welcomed and he also wondered if any of us would like to come on the actual challenge itself. He seemed like a really nice guy and a genuine kind of bloke who loved the outdoors passionately. He had a small group that he climbed with regularly and they trained mostly in Glendalough, meeting a couple of evenings a week in the upper car park.

'I'll chat to the crew here and see who's up for it. Sounds like a bit of craic. We'll see you next Saturday in Glendalough and, hey, if I think of anyone else I can round up, I'll bring them along too.' Emma, to her credit, was game from the off. The rest of them just laughed, looking at me as if they could sense another hairbrained scheme. Everyone in the office was still recovering from our charity book launches with Willow Ward. *Sure, how hard can it be?* I thought to myself. *A few hills? No big deal.* I drove that evening to the airport, excited to meet Desmond Llewellyn, the great Q from the James Bond movies, who was over on behalf of a client of mine, *Sláinte Health* magazine. I was thinking hard about who might be up for this bit of mountain devilment. I felt we needed someone from the media and someone senior from the corporate sector whose support would offer a degree of legitimacy and credibility to the whole challenge. Who better than someone successful in business and happiest out on the hills? I smiled to myself, 'I know just the man for the job!'

Oliver Tattan has had the unusual experience of being a senior public servant turned entrepreneur. He brought his own vision to the challenges facing public policymakers in driving economic growth, juxtaposed with the challenges faced by the entrepreneur in taking on liberalising markets. By the time I met him, he had already founded high-growth companies in the health care, financial services and software sectors (all in his late twenties and thirties). After a career spent in Germany, Brazil (he ended up marrying a Brazilian) and South Africa, he returned to Ireland to take a leading role in helping to continue developing our economic miracle, or Celtic Tiger as we were proudly calling it.

Then there was Paul Cullen from *The Irish Times*, known by readers for many good reasons. His utterly humane coverage of the tragic earthquake that occurred in Turkey some years back, his intelligent Tribunal reporting in print and on radio, and his sincere coherent style make him one of the very best journalists of his generation. He's also a very fine athlete and mountain runner! After speaking to him initially, Paul was very happy to come on board and support John's cause. So we had the makings of a small but happy team.

When I look back now, to that very first attempt at climbing the five peaks in 2002, I realise I was utterly clueless. To be fair, I didn't even know the names of the five mountains in question, let alone know where they were. I could only have named four in fact – England's peak in the Lake District remained a complete mystery to me.

1984: Ian (back row, fourth from right) joins his schoolmates celebrating their famous Schools U14 Gaelic Football title.

1986: Ian (bottom left) celebrates with Peter Dunne, Philip Dowling, Eamonn Sweetman and teacher Jim Byrne, the first time Clonkeen College won the prestigious 4 x 100 m Senior Schools National title.

1998: A trip to Anfield. Ian (right) joins Willow Ward (second from left) with Michael Owen and Steve McManaman, soon to leave for Real Madrid.

The team that climbed all 26 peaks North and South of Ireland in 98 hours and 45 minutes in June 2006: Ian (second from left), Laura Shilling (fifth from left) and Gerry Christie, PRO of the Kerry Mountain Rescue (last on right).

One of the many famous Santa Cycles between 1995 and 2004.
Pictured front with Ian are Stephen Peers and Gordon Ward.
Spot Miss Ireland, anyone?

The world's largest coin mural (made up of 1.6 million coins) to
celebrate the official changeover to the euro. It was organised by the
charity Operation Rudolph.

World Record No. 1: (l-r) Niall Kavanagh, Lorcan Sweetman, Ian McKeever and Cathal Gregg powering their way off Carrauntohill at 6.10 a.m. on 25 June 2004. They set a new record for the Five Peaks Challenge in a time of 16 hours and 16 mintues.

Ian high in the French Alps in training for the Seven Summits record attempt, August 2006.

Time out! Relaxing in Chamonix with (from left) cameraman John Whittle and 'Cossy', the man who does chin ups with his fingers!

Lorraine Keane joins Ian on the famous 2002 Five Peaks Challenge attempt. Pictured coming off Snowdon Mountain in Wales.

September 2006: Just some of the 5,000 calories a day Ian had to consume to prepare for his gruelling task ahead. Pictured here with his friend Paul Hughes at the Abbeyglen Hotel in Galway.

January 2007: Zorat (left) and Sean Swarner (right), the world's first cancer survivor to climb Everest with just one lung, join Ian at the base camp for a moment of relaxation at Patriot Hills.

February 2007: Roy Jardine (left) joins Ian and John at the camp at 4,200 metres on Aconcagua.

11 February 2007: Descending from his second mountain: Ian at 6,700 metres on Aconcagua.

11 February 2007: Ian summits his 'Everest': Aconcagua Mountain. Placing a school's flag at the 7,000-metre point.

Ian with Simon Braithwate at the top of the Vinson Massif on 25 January 2007.

To put things into some kind of perspective, training on my side consisted of changing absolutely nothing in my very bad diet, continuing to smoke (ten a day on average, twice that on the weekends) and turning up for training without any clue about real preparation, pre-hydration or even the running shoes on my feet. We used to train two to three times a week. I really hated the 500 steps that spiral upwards, menacingly past the Visitors' Centre opposite the second lake. Of course, there are actually more than 500 steps – it's quite a surprise when you begin to try and run up them. The first 100 or so lead you past the waterfall and on up to the upper path. If you are as unfit as I was back then, you will breakdown before you complete them. In those days, I'd struggle to the top and then light a cigarette for my troubles, sitting down breathing rather violently. At the time, I thought showing up would be enough – give the legs a chance to adjust and the heart would follow somehow. Looking back now, I can understand the look of disgust that would occasionally come over Paul's face when he'd see me struggling. I think he knew that I had potential buried somewhere in the recesses of my poor mistreated body.

Besides, I was more into the whole PR end of the gig, organising the photocalls, setting up the radio interviews, raising some money; that's where I felt most useful at the time.

Our route was to take us from Carrauntohill in County Kerry to Slieve Donard in County Down, whereupon myself and Emma were going to organise a spectacular parting of the Red Sea! The gardaí had very kindly agreed to give us an unbroken escort all the way to Dún Laoghaire port. This was an amazing undertaking by any stretch of the imagination. Our support drivers, like little puppy dogs salivating at the prospect of a juicy treat, were instructed to travel in tight convoy in between both garda bikes or cars depending on the particular stretch in question. They were told that their speed was not to drop below a certain limit (which was 90 mph on average!) and they were to follow exactly whatever signals the various gardaí gave.

I'll never forget coming into Dundalk, which at the time wasn't bypassed. People's jaws simply dropped, ice cream cones fell to the ground and children stood motionless as this bizarre convoy blew into town like the magnificent seven. The whole operation was astounding and the garda driving and co-ordinating skills displayed under pressure and at high speeds were a testament to their training. We made Dún Laoghaire in one hour and ten minutes, ashen-faced but giggling like children who'd just had their first rollercoaster ride. The trip across on the ferry was peaceful enough and we all put our heads down to sleep for a couple of hours in anticipation of the two-hour journey to Wales' highest peak.

Despite feeling rather stiff and sore after the first two mountains, I was in good spirits. There had been such a gap between the climbs that fitness critically wasn't playing any real part. Bedsides which, we had gone up both peaks at a reasonably leisurely pace of three and a half hours for Carrauntohill and three hours for Donard respectively. There had been lots of time to get plenty of food and drinks on board in the interim.

In Welsh, the summit of Snowdon is called *Yr Wyddfa*, which translates as a tomb or monument. Legend has it that it is the tomb of Rhita Gawr, an ogre who would kill kings and make cloaks out of their beards. He supposedly met his end when King Arthur climbed to the top of Snowdon and killed him. The mountain is truly beautiful and a spectacular climb. No one knows who first conquered it, but ascents of the mountain became very popular indeed after Thomas Pennant published *Tours* in 1781 and included details of his visit to the summit. The mountain, and the surrounding area, has been mined since the Bronze Age, and evidence of copper mining can be seen all over the place, from old mine buildings to old tramways. The peak itself stands at 1,085 metres (3,560 feet). Each year, an incredible 350,000 people reach the summit, some on foot and some by train. I was aghast on this, my first journey to the summit, to see a group of old-age pensioners getting off the train just moments from the actual summit. Blimey, I thought, maybe we should have done the same. My legs were really sore at this point and I was climbing without the aid of walking poles – very foolish indeed.

We were told by one of the locals that the actual summit gets over 200 inches of rain every year, can reach temperatures of 30°C in high summer and plummet to −20°C in the winter. Add to this winds of up to 150 mph and the temperature can feel more like −50°C. I have to admit that that particular peak was not one where I wanted to hang around. In fact, of the twelve or so trips I have made up Snowdon since, only once did the sun shine brightly at the top. On this particular occasion, I was still fascinated by the railway. How did they construct this wonderful feat of engineering?

Even though I was completely knackered coming off the mountain, I had thoroughly enjoyed the Welsh experience and felt something very spiritual about the place, even though I had no real concept of what that meant at the time.

Next up, the five-plus hour journey north to the Lake District and to the mountain I knew nothing about. The journey was good craic and everyone remained in high spirits. I could feel my legs stiffening up horribly, though, and the lactic acid was lodged in my calves like cement. 'Not sure I'm going to get much further,' I muttered to myself.

England's highest peak, Scafell Pike, stands 978 metres (3,208 feet) and is climbed by thousands of people each year. Along with Ben Nevis and Snowdon, it is one of the mountains climbed as part of the celebrated and hugely popular Three Peaks Challenge in Britain. The name 'The Pikes of Sca Fell' was applied to the peaks which are nowadays known as Scafell Pike, Ill Crag and Broad Crag. It was, in fact, an error on an ordinance survey map naming the highest Scafell Pike that has now stuck and is in common use. The neighbouring peak, Sca Fell, looks higher from many angles, but is actually just 10 feet lower. The mountain was donated to the British National Trust in the first quarter of the twentieth century by Lord Leconfield in memory of the men of the Lake District who died in the First World War.

There are two main routes up this challenging peak; the most popular starts from Wasdale Head Inn (itself famous as reputedly the birthplace of British climbing), and the other from Seathwaite in Borrowdale. The second is a longer route, but one which rewards the walker with magnificent views. Several years later, the Wasdale Head Inn would become a very important place for me but, on this occasion, I was simply keen to find out a little bit more about the history of this great mountain, never thinking I'd ever be coming back here. As John, Paul and Oliver began their trek, we found the locals were happy to inform us about a great many interesting facts. Emma and I were staying behind. My legs were shot and I was happy to light up and enjoy the views.

Later, Paul and Oliver informed me that the summit of Scafell Pike is strewn with boulders, and much of the walk up involves clambering over rocks and has uneven footing. It is a rugged, barren, grey peak with no vegetation. The route up Scafell Pike is far harder to follow than the paths up Snowdon or even Ben Nevis and needs a map and a compass. The area is crisscrossed with paths going in different routes and directions, and even in good weather, the lads informed me, it is not always possible to retain a sense of direction or to recognise, on the way back, the route you took to the summit. The path itself, though marked with cairns, often is not easy to follow. Boy was I glad I wasn't going up it on this particular occasion.

It was difficult to discover who *first* ascended Scafell Pike, but possibly easy to see why no particular note was made of the achievement. Unlike Snowdon or Ben Nevis, as I would later discover, which stand proudly distinct in their surroundings, offering a challenge to all who see them, Scafell Pike is not a peak that is clearly seen from a distance (perhaps that's why I wasn't really bothered to climb it!) and indeed looks no higher than any of its neighbours. However, that said, the highest mountain in England has drawn many to try to reach its summit for over two centuries. Josh Naylor, a very famous local now in his seventies (who would become very important in my life at a later stage), held the world's fastest time up and down the mountain, completing it in under an hour – fifty-seven minutes to be exact. This man has no cartilage in his right knee and for his sixtieth birthday set about climbing the sixty peaks in the Lake District that are above 2,000 feet. The DVD has to be seen to be believed.

Mountain climbs in the Lake District apparently became popular at the start of the eighteenth century. Our locals informed us that Samuel Taylor Coleridge visited and climbed the peak in 1802, which inspired Dorothy Wordsworth, sister of the famous poet William, to climb with her friend, maid, hired porter and shepherd guide in 1818. Although there doesn't seem to be a record of William himself climbing the peak, four years later, he used his sister's notes on the climb and published it himself. Dorothy states that the summit was 'gained after much toil, though without difficulty' which probably sums up most people's feelings of the ascent.

The time seemed to fly past. Before we knew it the lads were up and down in three and a half hours or so. Though the boys were tired, they remained focused on the job in hand. Everyone was, nevertheless, keen to keep the show on the road and so we began the six-hour journey north to our final destination and the mother of all ascents, Ben Nevis, standing proudly at 1,344 metres (4,406 feet) head and shoulders above all others peaks on these islands. If you can imagine a spiralling staircase that spins till infinity, then you have a pretty good idea of what it's like to climb this monstrosity of a mountain. The three lads were exhausted but absolutely determined to make it.

The photograph that appeared in the Monday edition of *The Irish Times* back in 2000 read proudly of the wonderful achievement of three men (John Morrison, Paul Cullen and Oliver Tattan) who had accomplished the Five Peaks of Britain and Ireland by land and sea in a new record time of forty-two hours. It seems incredible to think now that, as I lay in bed that morning, listening to Ian Dempsey joking about my absence from the photo, I would one day in fact dare to contemplate knocking thirty-one hours off that excellent time recorded by the lads.

It was perhaps inevitable that John would want to raise the bar to yet another level. What's incredible as I think about it now is that I didn't want to move with him. One year later, John was determined that we would do the very same challenge using a Sikorsky helicopter, enabling him to climb all five peaks in under twenty-four hours. Once again, my skills were best deployed in the planning, PR and fundraising end of things. I had suggested that, in order to raise more money for Focus Ireland, we should invite more guys like Oliver on board. To their great credit Guinness, O2, Country Manor Bricks and what was then BUPA coughed up the money needed between them – the equivalent back then of €12,000 per company. Siobhan Saunders who was brand manger at the time for Guinness Breó was chosen internally to represent their company on the climb. Mary Bernie, a pal of mine, was the other new female addition to the team and represented Country Manor Bricks. What would make this challenge all the more fascinating was the intention by John to make a documentary of it. There would be no RTÉ funding but, instead, a very brave effort to capture the mood, events and highlights of this attempt to scale the five peaks in a new record time. Other additions to the team included Pat Leahy from the *Sunday Business Post*.

The attempt to achieve the new record time failed in the end. A combination of factors conspired against us, not least the fact that the helicopter was late arriving to pick us up from Carrauntohill Mountain due to poor weather conditions. Nevertheless, the resulting documentary which was shot on a hand-held camera by two friends of John's, Cait and Martina, made for riveting viewing thanks in no small part to an excellent edit back at base. Once again, I broke down after three mountains. This time, I failed to even get up Snowdon. I can still recall how dehydrated my body had become in the heat coming off Slieve Donard late that morning and I never really recovered. In fact, if it wasn't for John's persistence, I'd never even have made it off that mountain either. I simply hadn't come around to the idea of training properly. I had no comprehension of what it took to prepare myself and I got what I richly deserved – a very rude awakening when I saw the resulting piece of film. It was Mary Bernie, however, who stole the show. Mary had twisted her ankle on Carrauntohill and was simply unable to continue after coming off Donard. Even today, I find myself responding to the tears in her eyes as she tells her story. Not even the brilliant Paul Cullen could rescue the situation in the end. A small group of them (Paul, Pat, Siobhan and John) very bravely continued on despite being out of time in order to complete the challenge itself.

They called the short film *Five High*. Over the next couple of years, RTÉ showed it at least half a dozen times. The fact that it had one of the highest ever ratings for the entire *Would You Believe?* series probably helped of course. How incredible that this piece of film done on a shoestring budget and a lot of goodwill could have made such an impression. Not for the first time, RTÉ appreciated that people were fascinated with man's struggle with nature and the human journey that we must go on first. The viewing figures had proved it.

What made the situation all the more bizarre was the fact that, subsequently, an English millionaire by the name of Brian Scowcroft had led a team that set an official Guinness World Record time of nineteen hours and fifty-two minutes. The challenge had suddenly gone to a whole new level.

I approached Focus Ireland and suggested to them that a Four Peaks challenge in Ireland might be a good idea as a corporate fundraising scheme. Some of you may have even done the challenge since...

I remember later, sitting rather embarrassed at home with a pal of mine, watching a recording of *Five High*. I'm not sure if it was actually seeing me perform like that on television or the news of the official world record that sparked me, but that night I made a decision, a promise to myself if you will. I was going to break that world record. I was going to train properly. I was going to quit smoking and drinking. I was going to find out just how good I could be. I knew, however, that in order to do all of this I would need help – lots of help!

I approached John about going back, putting a new team together and trying again. I'm not sure exactly why John decided to opt out in the spring of 2002. I guess he had his reasons. He certainly didn't think that breaking the record was on. I must admit, at the time, I wondered myself, but, thankfully, a series of events were about to unfold that would change everything. There would simply be no going back from this point.

7

All for One and One for All

'Be faithful in small things because it is in them that your strength lies.'
Mother Theresa

I believe it was the Greek philosopher Euripides who remarked that prosperity is full of friends; but real friendship is shown in times of trouble. There are good reasons why most of us can count on only a few genuine friends. It is certainly true that when things start to go wrong, many people find an excuse to stop calling. To my mind, it takes people of exceptional character to stand up and be counted when you need them, for they are the exception rather than the norm.

Had Cathal Cregg not taken the meeting by the scruff of the neck that particular evening back in the spring of 2002, it's most likely I wouldn't be sitting here writing this book today. To be fair, he did me the courtesy of at least waiting till I had finished speaking before he addressed us. 'Well one thing's very much for sure. You won't have any problem publicising this mountain disaster either!'

Everyone just sat there gobsmacked. I thought we'd cracked it. I'd brought in the army, literally, to help us get fit and ready for this challenge. Two lieutenants, Neil Deegan (who had been responsible for training frightened army cadets and getting them fit as fools in the mountains) was on board and so too was Ireland's first female pilot in the Air Corps, Anne Brogan. I'd brought in a cool sponsor, Wrangler Jeans, who were going to be represented on the Five Peaks attempt by their marketing manager Pat O'Sullivan, and several well-known faces had agreed to come on board to give the media plenty to talk about, including Lorraine Keane and John Ryan, the man who had made *VIP* magazine famous. John had been brought on board by special request from Anne Strain who was in charge of fundraising for the Alzheimer Society for whom we had decided to do the Five Peaks Challenge under the guise of Operation Rudolph. Anne is a very capable operator and I wasn't going to say no to John as he'd already been on one of our previous Santa cycles.

Add to this lot a set of four brothers – the Sweetman family – all of whom were taking part. Lorcan was the eldest and the fittest; followed by Eamonn who had run with me on the 4 x 100-metre school relay team in 1986, that won Clonkeen College its first ever national title; Paul was the wise-cracking one that lived with me at the time; and Pat who was the youngest, the cute guy that the girls all loved.

So what was Cathal's point? I wondered. It didn't take too long to find out.

Because of Neil's hard work, we were fit and even though Lorraine was coming on board late in the day, I knew she'd be more than capable of getting there in the end. But there was something missing in our overall approach. We weren't really performing as a team. Cathal felt that there was far too much *'mé féining'* going on. Looking back, he was right. He spoke with Neil and, between them, they tweaked the training regime.

One particular evening, for example, Cathal decided that we were just going to concentrate on the first sixty steps that lead up from the waterfall. No more. The idea was that we would run in relay teams up and down the sets of steps. First one set, then two sets, and so on until the overall complement of six rows were completed. However, you were only allowed to run as fast as the slowest person in your team. The session was punishing and the very evident male ego struggled to comply. It was an excellent lesson in teamwork. Suddenly, the whole operation was beginning to have genuine meaning for me. I was starting to feel that I was part of something special. Each person on that team was assigned a 'buddy' that night. So we would be responsible for each other going forward in every sense of the word. This wasn't just about the training, but rather the other person's actual well-being. Every aspect of this challenge would now be divided up equally, from logistics and planning to PR and promotion.

To that end, we had an excellent person working with us as the administrator for Operation Rudolph, Cian Browne, who together with the very talented Jules McDonald from the well-respected firm of O'Leary PR (the agency looking after the PR needs of Wrangler), set about co-ordinating the whole promotional side of the gig. After an excellent launch in Reynard's nightclub, there was plenty of media interest in the record attempt. I approached Paddy Power bookmakers who gave the public odds on the various challenge participants. When the odds of 200–1 were announced for Lorraine Keane to complete the challenge, some serious money was placed.

To Lorraine's credit, she began to train after her entertainment shifts in TV3 were over. Sometimes, it could be as late as 9 p.m. before we got to do any training but she never missed a session. People had no idea at the time just how tough she is. In the early days of training, she had joined us on a 'rekkie' of Snowdon Mountain in Wales, where she struggled to keep pace. Neil Deegan rang Cathal the following day concerned. Cathal informed Neil that Lorraine was the least of his worries and that he'd take personal responsibility to ensure she'd be OK.

The media interest at the time was split between the 'celebrity' and the human interest. The tabloids followed Lorraine, Anne and John, while the broadsheets/radio, etc. took a firmer interest in everyone else, particularly the Sweetmans. I had known the guys since school and had only moved in the year previously with Paul, who ran a major computer supplies company that was located conveniently beside TV3 out in Ballymount. Paul and I got on exceptionally well – we both believed in working and playing hard. We also both agreed to quit smoking at the same time and went on similar training regimes.

I had decided to start using supplements and was doing weights for the first time. Back then, my weights programme was very unsophisticated and you'd never find me, for example, in the free weights room, probably because I'd drop them! I was too busy trying to burn 1,000 calories in forty-five minutes or less on the cross trainer, the one piece of apparatus that I found properly toned and worked the whole body, most especially the core.

I sometimes tell my PR students today that, along with 'depression' and 'schizophrenia', the words 'supplements' and 'creatine' are two of the most misunderstood and misused words in the entire English language. Think of it this way, if you don't have a chef making your meals for you at home and you train hard, you will most likely need to 'supplement' your daily diet with a balance of different things, ranging from sufficient levels of minerals and vitamins to additional protein and sufficient carbohydrate intake. Creatine is a naturally occurring organic acid in the human body that helps to supply energy to muscle and nerve cells. When kids are younger with higher metabolisms, there is no need to supplement an already naturally high production output, which is why teenagers should not take creatine, for example.

In my case, the training guys in the Crunch Fitness gym in Dún Laoghaire, where I had started training, had recommended the Maxi Muscle range to me. I wasn't especially enamoured at the time with the name! (In time, I would become very grateful for their eventual sponsorship of me and the wonderful help afforded me down the line by Ciaran Collins and his nutritionist Aoife.) Nevertheless, when I explained my basic needs, it was decided that I would use a product called Cyclone, an all-in-one formula that combined a daily serving of 60 grams of whey protein, 10 grams of creatine monohydrate and twenty-plus grams of carbohydrates, along with a whole range of other things that promised rapid results over a short period of time – ten pounds of lean muscle in four to six weeks.

Whilst, at the time, I may not have understood what every aspect was for, I had very quickly come to realise that if you train hard cardiovascularly and do weights as well, you more than likely need to supplement your daily diet. The reality is that the daily male requirement on average of 1 gram of protein for every pound of body weight cannot be met just through food intake, save eating four whole chickens every day! Besides which, I was not a good cook and there was a health shop called La Sante Health located on the ground floor of the Dún Laoghaire Shopping Centre beside the gym that sold what I needed.

In fact, I didn't cook period. If it couldn't be done in simple machines like blenders, juicers or microwaves, then I didn't do it. Paul on the other hand cooked very well. Sunday lunch in our house was, to be fair, quite a treat. Not to be outdone, Paul too decided to take supplements, despite his vast knowledge about fruit and vegetables.

We were renting a house at the time on the salubrious Convent Road in Dalkey. From the off, we had what we called the 'head and shoulders' effect on our neighbours. To the right were two elderly ladies, who didn't particularly like me but disliked Paul even more. They would often complain about the noise levels coming from number thirty-eight and call the guards from time to time. Paul was always polite to them, which probably annoyed them even more. Our other neighbours, however, did like us – a lot. Living to our left was a wonderful woman about our age, who lived with her daughter, whom I adored, and her mum.

Suffice to say, our party life went on complete hold for a three-month period in 2002. Going for a run the first night you quit smoking is ill-advised. I'll never forget the burning sensation I felt in my lungs and the disgusting taste of bile forming in mouth. I swore that I'd never smoke again (promises, promises!). If I ran ten minutes that night, then it's probably a bit of an exaggeration. But I was stubborn and I never broke a promise. Now that I had decided to get myself into gear and comply with the real training needs that Lieutenant Deegan had laid down, I was wholly determined to make the grade. I rapidly discovered that the real cardio training is done outdoors, on the hills, or, in the words of the great Muhammad Ali, 'The fight is won or lost away from witnesses, behind the lines, in the gym and out there on the road.'

In fact, several nights spent climbing Camaderry Hill would lead to vastly improved performances on the cross trainer. I was lighter, too, in those days. For the Five Peaks Challenge, it was all about being the right 'fighting' weight. I was five foot ten and weighed in at twelve stones and seven pounds on the day we began the challenge, with less than 9 per cent body fat. Within three weeks of training, my metabolism had speeded up remarkably and I was burning calories to beat the band. Both Paul and I noticed a rapid surge in our food intake. But, amazingly, and unlike the previous challenges, my body was crying out for only good foods. It had become more alkaline and was being flushed regularly with water, about three litres a day. We had both got into the Sonia O'Sullivan trick of starting the morning with a drop of warm water and lemon.

We lost our taste for alcohol as the endorphins began to kick in. Within just six weeks, the basic building blocks had been laid and our muscles had started to become conditioned for the real outdoor work that lay ahead. Camaderry Hill was starting to become my new best friend. Despite the long drive down (longer in those days before the alignment of the M50 bypass with the N11), I was starting to actually look forward to our training sessions. Located directly across from the second car park in Glendalough, the hill is impressive and the gradient is forty degrees. The hill climbs rapidly upwards for 800 feet breaking across a pathway, meandering swiftly through two forests before levelling somewhat at the top, where the deer can be seen crossing in the late evening. In simple terms, there is no better way to bring your heart rate down than working this hill. Initially, the considered overall group pace (eleven people climbing together) would dictate the group to be up in less than eleven minutes each time. As the sessions became tougher, the time dropped to ten minutes and the group would climb in succession up to five or six times in a row.

The trickiest part of the preparation for our pending assault on the Five Peaks record attempt lay in the logistics. As this had now become an official Guinness world record attempt, certain criteria had to be complied with. All data for the challenge had to be collated. This included press coverage, witness statements on each mountain to ensure that the correct times had been given, and journey logs for the participants and the pilots of the helicopters as, apart form anything else, there were certain grid references we had to comply with for landing purposes.

In order to help generate funds for the charity, all participants agreed to raise the equivalent of €12,000, with the exception of the army personnel who would raise less due to the support they were giving in other ways. For example, thanks to Neil and Anne, I had procured the support of the Air Corps press office who had generously agreed to provide us with one of their helicopters free of charge. On one of training nights, we were even visited by an Air Corps colonel who dropped in to share his insights and offer good advice.

Then on 20 June, the day before the challenge was due to take place, disaster struck. The Air Corps informed us that they would have to withdraw their helicopter as it was going to be needed for a training mission out west. We were frantic. Cian was on the phone to every helicopter operator in Ireland and Britain looking for support. Lorraine even went on the *Gerry Ryan Show* to put out an SOS. It was all to no avail. Half of the team had already been over in Scotland for several days preparing for the midnight start with the Scottish Mountain Rescue boys who had kindly agreed to lead us up the Nevis in the dark. Only myself and Lorraine were left to fly over.

John Ryan had started to become visibly agitated, and questioned why we couldn't now find a second helicopter. I believe this is where his famous line, 'I didn't sign up for this!' was first spoken. It was simply impossible, especially given the short notice.

In the end, Cian and I spoke with an operator in Glasgow, who was prepared to facilitate us with a twin-engine Bell 206, a much slower model compared with the Augusta 109 we had commissioned. But it was that or nothing and we were up against it. In short, using this helicopter was going to be very costly and would put extra pressure on the team to deliver faster times on the actual mountains. I spoke to Neil and Cathal and it was decided in the end that we had a real chance still to make it. The times we had practised with the team before this had always allowed for things going wrong. If the worst case scenario were to happen and we were behind schedule after the third mountain, we would take the fastest crew on the Augusta.

Rather frazzled, I joined the team later that afternoon. I could feel the tense atmosphere and allowed to myself become deeply upset that something like this was causing a rift in the team. At that time, I took things way too personally and internalised feelings that, in reality, had little to do with me. To everyone's credit, however, everything was forgotten as soon as *The Shawshank Redemption* began playing on the video player in the house we had rented, several miles from Nevis. This was the agreed choice of movie which everyone felt would inspire us. As Lorraine Keane joked, 'It's amazing how easy a bunch of lads are satisfied.'

And so the next evening, rested and filled with our final plate of carbo-loading pasta and chicken we set off into the dark for whatever lay ahead. The whole operation was filmed on hand-held video cam. Paul Sweetman took initial charge of filming, a decision he would later regret coming off Nevis, when he wasted too much energy running back and forth to capture everyone's progress.

Things went swimmingly to begin with. Lorraine and Anne took their time. You could smell the male testosterone wafting in the chilly Scottish air as the lads competed ferociously to outdo one another on the descent of the biggest mountain in the British Isles. It was all Cathal could do not to laugh as he watched the boys falling over one another. Meanwhile the girls were oblivious, concentrating instead on their breathing and pace. It was a beautiful morning. The sun had risen to greet us at the bottom. As we entered the valley below, you could hear the engines of the two helicopters starting to rev and groan. Everyone was in terrific spirits boarding. The lightweight platypus packs, which we carried on our backs for hydration purposes, were working a treat and everyone appeared to be sipping their isotonic/water combined drinks and eating lots of carbohydrates and sugars in accordance with the diet plans that had been done for us.

We tore up and down Scafell Pike. I couldn't believe it. I had rekkied the mountain just once before with Neil. I'll never forget embarrassing him that time, when upon reaching the col (also called a pass or saddle), I asked a group of people if were going the right way through the thick mist and fog that was forming. Meanwhile, Neil was busy taking a compass reading.

I knew that the third mountain was going to suit us all very well. Snowdon allows an initial run in of about a mile or so after the helicopter has landed just before the first lake. We were all brimming with energy and happy by that point to start running at the speed of the slowest man. It was indeed a man, Pat Sullivan, who really was doing just fine. The weather had remained on our side. Good tail winds and glorious sunshine had prevailed all the way into Wales. Once again, the team performed brilliantly, eating up the ground up and down. As we got back into the helicopters, we were a whole two hours up on the record time. What could possibly burst our bubble?

Slieve Donard, which peaks at 850 metres, is the highest mountain in 'nine-county Ulster' and strangely enough only the nineteenth highest in Ireland. It's named after St Domhangart, a contemporary of St Patrick, and stands next to the picturesque seaside town of Newcastle. It's an interesting climb, not only because of the spectacular views it offers to those who make the effort, but because of the climb itself. The trek up the mountain is marked out with a rocky path, including steps up the mountain. When you reach the saddle, you turn left and follow the 150-foot Mourne Wall to the top of the mountain. It's an excruciating section of climb in poor weather, prevailing winds and very tired limbs.

This is exactly where everything changed on our Five Peaks Challenge record attempt. The testosterone levels evaporated and nearly every single guy on the challenge was in deep trouble. Lorraine and Anne stopped halfway up to offer John Ryan a sandwich. He didn't really smile back, but he did help Paul Sweetman who was struggling badly. The meaning of teamwork finally hit this team like a boxer who had just been sucker punched in the fourteenth round. The Mourne Wall can provide great shelter from wind and rain on a cold day, but it does very little to restore the power back into your legs. We huddled together for shelter, everyone now acutely aware of their 'buddy'. Getting off the mountain was a painstaking exercise in nerve and will. I was one of the slowest coming down as my knees felt like they were on fire. Once again, I had chosen (for the last time admittedly) to climb without the aid of walking sticks, unlike the girls who offered words of encouragement as they sauntered past me.

By the time we had crawled back on to the helicopters, we had lost our two hours in hand. Suddenly, we were up against it. The pilots then informed us of poor weather coming in from the south. Conditions on Carrauntohill were at best going to be touch and go. Poor old Paul chucked whatever he had left on the helicopter but at least he tried to laugh about it.

Landing at Cronin's Yard, we knew the record was looking more and more unlikely, yet we were determined to finish even if were going to be outside the record time. We headed across the river point, up the valley for the infamous Devil's Ladder, that 100-metre section of scree and loose rock that stands perilously between the climber and likely glory on the summit. It was clear on the final approach that we weren't going to be able to go any further. We were exactly one hour outside the record. The rain was belting down and high winds were gusting all around us. The narrow streams had joined up and the scene resembled a cascading river rushing its way to the 300-foot drop to the bottom of the ladder.

We had been scrambling tirelessly for twenty hours and temperaments were frail. Eamonn Sweetman was the first to let his feelings be known. He thought we should risk it and continue on. Great debates ensued but there could only be one outcome. There were, however, bigger problems to surmount.

As with every other peak, Cathal had meticulously planned support at the base and closer to the peak of each mountain in compliance with the record authority's wishes that all ascents be logged and filed. So, up ahead in dreadful conditions, two guys were waiting for us. One, John Darcy, an experienced climber, was bedded down in his tent close to the actual summit whilst the other, younger and wearing less protective clothing, was perched dangerously on the Devil's Ladder itself. Talks ensued between Cathal and Neil as to what needed to be done. This young guy needed to be rescued and we needed to get the bulk of the exhausted team off the mountain. Mickey Brennan, a friend of Cathal's, led the team reluctantly back to shelter at Cronin's Yard, a tricky operation as the river had become extremely dangerous to cross. Cathal and Neil contacted the Kerry Mountain Rescue and waited for their arrival where the cobbled route intersects below the Ladder. Anne to her eternal credit managed to get us a lift back to the Baldonnell air strip courtesy of the Air Corps who made a plane available to take us back at four in the morning. We all fell into bed that evening, assuming that that would be the end of what we considered to be a heroic effort to break the record.

Just how I found myself on the *Joe Duffy Show* two days later remains a bit of an embarrassment. Perhaps I felt some misplaced need to defend the actions of those involved with the Five Peaks Challenge or perhaps I simply leaped before thinking it through properly. Either way, it's a decision I do regret.

The previous day, Gerry Christie the PRO for the Kerry Mountain Rescue (who would give us great support in the future), had gone on air to highlight the facts of what had ensued the previous night. He was critical of the clothing worn by the person on the ladder ('Shoes were like something you'd find in Ballymagash!' I believe is how he phrased it) and there was a distinct sense he felt that we had abandoned people on the mountain. I felt if nothing else I needed to give the listeners a sense of why this person was actually being rescued and some background to the whole story. Nobody had been abandoned, quite the opposite. Either way, the story gathered pace and before you know it, we were all over the papers as a result of the initial story breaking on *Joe Duffy*.

I always remember Margaret O'Reilly back in the 1990s, when she was the manager of the Northern Ireland Tourist Board, being asked about the difficulties in marketing Northern Ireland in the light of the ongoing Troubles. She referred to the fact that people have short memories and thankfully learn to move on. In our case, all that people remembered of the record attempt was the disaster at the top of Carrauntohill.

There were some very harsh but important lessons to be learned in the aftermath of that particular challenge. If you court the media to support you, then you must accept they have every right to question you when things go wrong. If you decide to go ahead with an expensive operation, regardless of the reasons why at the time, you need to make sure you have all the money in on the other side first.

Not long after the challenge was over, I received a phone call to say that the new record for the Five Peaks stood at an incredible sixteen hours and forty-eight minutes. As I took in this astonishing information, the words that I had spoken to the group that night in the torrential rain at the foot of the Devil's Ladder echoed in mind: 'We live to fight another day. I'm going to go back. Whoever wants to join me can. We will make this right.'

Taking out a cigarette, I sat back and pondered my next move.

8

Putting the Record Straight

'Our lives begin to end the day we become silent about things that matter.'
Martin Luther King

They say, don't they, that you should never go back. Never revisit the past, for fear of the consequences, the hurt and, of course, the likely anger. What makes us want to go back in the first place? Is it a sense of misplaced pride; we can't let go of that partner or thing that we clung on to, desperately afraid to let go, for so long? Maybe there's a perceived sense of wrongdoing and, by going back, we feel that we can right those wrongs. Perhaps we're just simply too headstrong to let our sleeping dogs lie.

Who are *they* anyway? Perhaps they represent those wise souls who themselves learned the painful lessons along the way, that one day others might heed... According to the celebrated writer and philosopher Eckhart Tolle, there is only the present in which we can truly live.

Cathal said he had half-expected my call. He was ready for it. He reckoned that any man who was prepared to leave Dublin and live in the mountains was serious about going back. We met up in late autumn 2003 in a pizzeria on Dublin's Baggot Street. Cigarette in mouth, I cut quickly to the chase: 'This is the last cigarette you will see me smoke and the last time you will ever hear me mention the Five Peaks Challenge. We need a team of four and we go back next summer to put things right. Are you in?' The question was rhetorical.

Of course, the Cajun, as he was known, was going back. There was a steely determination in his blue eyes as he replied, 'Mc, let's put this record straight once and for all.' Cathal was an inspiration.

Putting the record straight began with my move out of Dublin in the summer of 2003. Incredibly, I'd never really lived on my own. Since breaking up with my ex-wife, Marguerite, some five or six years earlier, there had been two serious relationships in my life – with Sue and Sandra – and I had co-habited in both cases and, for the rest of the time, I'd shared with Paul, living the good life in Dalkey. It was time for a change, a chance to stand on my own two feet for once.

Lorcan Sweetman, who had taken part in the 2002 Five Peaks Challenge, was the next man to join us. Lorcan was arguably one of the fittest guys I'd ever met. He was tall and there was not an ounce of fat on him. He worked as the building/projects officer in UCD and training was simply part of who he was. Most of his lunch breaks were spent running on the dirt track with colleagues. Anne, Lorcan's wife, had a dozen or so cats, while Lorcan was more of a dog man himself. Often you might see Charlie, his half-collie mix, scampering alongside him as he ran the Spinc, or up along the side of Scar Mountain on an autumn's evening.

Anne and Lorcan kindly offered me the chance to rent a charming one-up, one-down 'Hansel and Gretel'-style residence that Lorcan had built single-handedly. It was in the grounds of the gorgeous bungalow that he had also restored to perfection and in which he lived with Anne. Even though Lorcan and I were very different people, we actually got on very well as friends. The moment that I saw the cottage, nestled peacefully on the upper road to Lough Dan, I knew I had found a place to just simply be.

Lough Dan is without doubt one of the most spiritual and peaceful locations anywhere in Ireland. You just have to look at the car registrations from all over to see how far people travel for weekend visits at every opportunity, and to fully appreciate just how popular this serene spot is. The lake itself, located about a mile or so from where I was moving to was eerily beautiful and a wonderful place to simply chill and relax. There was also the famous scouting den set on some twenty acres around the lake itself and used by the many scouting groups from all over Ireland and abroad.

Then, there were lots and lots of exciting hill runs to consider. I felt a little bit like Rocky in *Rocky IV*, where he sets up his training camp deep in the heart of Mother Russia. And whilst nobody had died in my case, I nevertheless felt this huge inexplicable need to make good on the heroic efforts of those who had joined me the last time, only to be denied an hour from likely success at the foot of the Devil's Ladder. As I surveyed all around me that evening, delighted to be moving in, the only real question remaining was, who would fill the fourth place on the next attempt?

Eamonn and Neil had moved on to bigger mountains and were planning several long-term projects, including Elbrus, Europe's highest mountain, and, eventually, Aconcagua, South America's tallest peak in Argentina. My long-standing buddy, Lorraine, with whom I spoke to at length, was about to get married to her partner, Pete Devlin, whose band, the Devlins, had been busy recording their next album. Of course I would have loved Lorraine to come back but, to be fair, the type of training now required would have placed unacceptable demands on her time, and her body for that matter. She was happy to opt out.

In the end, we didn't have to look too far, thankfully. Niall Kavanagh, a long-standing pal and business colleague of Cathal's, was only too happy to volunteer. A champion swimmer and talented marathon runner from Laois, this man had the pedigree and no shortage of hunger. His lovely wife, Madeline, and even their kids were right behind him from the start. Most importantly, Niall, despite excelling in solo sports, was a genuine team player. Without any shadow of doubt, if we were going to have any chance of breaking the new world record of sixteen hours and forty-eight minutes, we were going to have to all reach not only exceptional levels of fitness but forge a bond that would see us through the worst of times.

Having been stung by one of the team members last time out, in terms of us providing the financial support for the charity, and following the additional embarrassment with the Air Corps, there was only one way we could do this viably and that was to secure the money for the helicopter upfront. The helicopter now required was an Augusta 109, capable of incredibly fast speeds and the same model used by the existing record holders from the UK.

Help came in the form of a man I had met previously through my work with the Alzheimer Society of Ireland and who managed very successfully Shire Pharmaceuticals, a company that focused its business on a tight range of disease areas: attention deficit and hyperactivity disorder, human genetic therapies and gastrointestinal and renal diseases. One of its core interest areas in Ireland was a treatment for delaying and reducing the symptoms of Alzheimer's. I had met the dynamic man behind the success of Shire in Ireland, Brian Martin, on a number of occasions and felt comfortable about approaching him for his support. The guy was incredibly talented and driven and had pretty much single-handedly helped to turn what had begun life as a one-man operation repping on the dusty roads on behalf of its mothership in the UK into a very serious pharmaceutical player here in Ireland. Given that we wanted to support the ASI on this final attempt, Brian went out on a limb to find us the money. Shire was much smaller than many of its competitors, such as Pfizer, and operated in a disease area in which it was a small fish in much larger pond. As a result, budgets were tight.

However, Brian realised that, corporately, this was an interesting and novel thing for the company to be associated with.

Although training for the 2004 Five Peaks Challenge can hardly be compared in overall terms with what was to come down the line, it was nevertheless savage in its intensity and commitment. Upper body weights were virtually shelved in favour of some serious leg work. Cardiovascularly, things were about to be taken to a whole new level.

I had many faults that needed to be addressed at the time. One of those related to my poor posture. Reluctantly, I had gone to see a chiropodist under the recommendation of Anne Strain to have some of my issues assessed. In simple terms, I had flat feet; Plantar Syndrome was a regular heartache anytime I tried to run serious miles. My right leg was longer and though it is not unusual to have one leg longer than the other, mine was more than five millimetres longer, and that's three millimetres more than the norm. And so I was fitted for orthotics, which were, in turn, specially fitted for my Nike running shoes by one of the country's top chiropodists Joe Byrne, who is based in Tallaght. Just several doors up from Joe was another amazing character who was to prove more than a life-saver during these intensive training sessions, the great 'AK' or Alan Kelly, sports physio to the stars.

This might seem a little clichéd but the moment you walk into Alan's waiting room, there are amazing pictures on the walls of just about anyone who's anyone in sport. One of my favourite pictures is a photo of Dessie Farrell being tackled by Enda McNulty, taken from the classic 2002 All-Ireland semi-final between Dublin and Armagh. McNulty's right hand is caught in the face of Dessie's and the caption below reads: 'Ulster says no!' Harrington, O'Driscoll, Carey. The sport didn't seem to matter; they came in their droves to be helped. It's fair to say that sometimes the simple difference between playing at all might be the excruciating sessions spent on this man's table. Forget Swedish massage, you didn't understand the word pain until Kelly's hands had worked you over!

One of the key requirements in any sport at any reasonable level is to have a strong and solid core. Yes, I'm referring in part to the defined six-pack muscles. To strengthen mine and help improve my general overall flexibility, I turned to a great friend of mine, Aisling Forkin, who strongly suggested in the pub one night that I consider learning the basic movements associated with Astanga Yoga. Aisling had tired of the corporate world and had decided to become a yoga teacher, wanting more out of life than a simple pay cheque at the end of the week.

For those of you who take a strong interest in the area, I think it's only fair to share some observations and to try and do some justice to the important role I believe yoga can play generally in our lives. Contrary to popular myths about yoga, in the Sanskrit (the foundational language of Hinduism), the word 'yoga' ties in with many of the spiritual disciplines of the Hindu religion. There is evidence of the practice of spiritual yoga dating as far back as the Vedas, or Hindu Bible, if you will. In fact, the words 'yoga' and 'religion' essentially carry the same definition – i.e. 'to yoke' ('yuj/yoga') to the spirit and 'to link or bind' ('religio') to the spirit. The term 'Astanga', referring to the type of yoga I was undertaking, is now something of an abused term, with many referring to it naively as some form of 'Power Yoga'! It actually refers to the eight-fold progression of classical/traditional (Dharma) yoga.

So, given the delicate and complex nature of understanding and overall appreciation associated with yoga generally, why was I then so keen to explore the associated benefits given that I was a complete novice and knew little or nothing about it?

Firstly, there were the direct and obvious benefits, and, if I could master the basics even reasonably, they would help me enormously. Astanga yoga is marked by a series of postures (many graceful, sometimes intricate) that flow together to create constant movement. Two of the core practical benefits are muscular endurance and flexibility. Even those with a strong basic level of fitness can often find it difficult to complete every pose the first time out, especially if upper-body strength is lacking. Significantly, however, yoga is about bringing a sense of harmony to the body by helping to balance hormones. How does it do this and why does it matter? You cannot talk about yoga without appreciating the meditative dimension. Meditation in simple terms is about paying attention, and keeping focused on one particular thing, be it the breath, sound, movement or what is referred to in yoga parlance as 'Asana' (body posture).

This relaxed focus of mind brings balance to the cortical, or brain activities, nervous system and endocrine system, which reduces and, in effect, helps to harmonise certain stress hormones, such as adrenaline, noradrenaline and cortisol. The result, in layman's terms, is a calmer and more peaceful state of body and mind. In fact, the word 'hormone' comes from the word 'harmony', so these are effectively the substances which keep body and mind in harmony with environment and nature.

However, the real secret for me was learning how to breathe and the importance of how we actually breathe. These learning curves would, unbeknownst to me, become essential tools much later, when I found myself stranded at the top of the world.

I was shocked when I started working with Aisling to discover the wasteful and 'shallow' manner in which I had been breathing up to that point. Being a former smoker hadn't helped matters, of course. The process of breathing is subconscious, and is not necessarily happening in a balanced and efficient manner. When was the last time you took a conscious breath?

Pranayama, a limb of yoga practice or specifically, in my case, what they call, the Ujjayi breath, helped to strengthen my diaphragmatic area and so work my core. It taught me to bring a mental consciousness, if you will, to the normally subconscious activity of breathing in order to make my breathing more efficient. This, in turn, helped to balance the oxygen, carbon dioxide and other soluble gas levels in my blood. Through this consciousness, Aisling taught me for the first time how my mind can help to control my body. In yogic terms being able to control the mind is essential for concentration. In practical terms, for all of us in this crazy world, greater mental control helps to bring a degree, at least, of emotional control and balance and mental clarity.

In addition, this breathing technique aims to improve the efficiency of oxygenation of the blood. Think about it for a moment. We all tend to take short shallow breaths, right? A situation which is always exaggerated when we are stressed or emotional. During this shallow breathing, it is estimated that the average person uses only between half and two thirds of their lung capacity, with the remaining healthy lung area unused. We also recycle some of the waste carbon dioxide when we breathe like this and so reduce the amount of new oxygen for the alveoli. This means that by breathing more optimally, each breath can transfer up to 50 per cent more oxygen into the blood to feed the body. It doesn't take a genius therefore to appreciate the extreme importance and value of actual breathing. Just think about it in the relative context of food and water. Without food, the body may survive for a certain number of weeks; without water, we might make it for a few days. But without air… we are lost.

The sessions were tough. It took me about five sessions to get some upper-body strength which, in turn, helped me with some of the postures and moves but the benefits by week ten, when considered in tandem with a controlled diet and structured training plan, were immense. I rapidly changed to one-to-one sessions with Aish.

The series of test results which followed in Trinity College in the spring of 2004, to test my fitness levels were, overall, very encouraging. I needed proper monitoring and assessing not only so that I could benchmark myself but also to see how empirical evidence can support your chosen training regimes.

I'll always remember, however, Bernard, the man who oversaw the programme, joking with me the first time I stood on the treadmill waiting for the harness and breathing apparatus to be placed on my face, about my next visit to the Rotunda and when my baby was due!

On the machine, they increase the running pace every three minutes by one kilometre an hour and prick your finger for a blood sample to assess the key performance indicators such as your lactate thresholds expressed in aerobic and anaerobic outputs and your VO_2 max (which defines your maximum rate of oxygen consumption). It is a measure, therefore, of your actual capacity to generate the energy required for endurance activities and is one of the most important factors determining your ability to exercise for longer.

For VO_2 max improvement to occur, training runs should be conducted usually at an intensity of at least 70 per cent of VO_2 max and closer to 100 per cent as you improve. In effect, you are conducting interval training, which is the method practised and favoured by the Swedish cross-country skiers. So the next time you step on the cross trainer in your gym, consider the following basics which might help you get more out of your training sessions. With the cross trainer (helpful for people with poor knees who can't run miles), you get to work the key muscle groups, most especially the core. Your overall programme should be based on the simple principle of resistance over time. Naturally, like me, you'll discover that you can't travel faster without first learning to travel for longer and then as you get fitter in aerobic terms, you can look at increasing the speeds for short periods of three- to five-minute intervals within the sessions and allowing a similar recovery time in between. Your speed on a cross trainer is indicated by the rpms. At my best, I was able to burn a typical 1,000 machine-indicated calories in approximately forty-five minutes.

Interestingly enough, on the first set of tests done by Bernard, when I'd just gone back to training, my anaerobic threshold was a very poor but expected 14.5 kilometres per hour. Three and a half years later, I would be running at that speed for an entire average sixty-minute session. My anaerobic threshold, or point at which I would bottom out, at the height of my physical exertions increased in the next three years by a full 3.5 kilometres per hour to a more impressive 18 kilometres. In other words, I could run considerably harder for longer and became faster overall thanks to proper interval training.

But most of my sessions back in the spring of 2004, particularly with the lads, were being done on the hills, concentrating on the endurance and the leg and mind conditioning. At the peak period of my training, several weeks before we tapered off for our rest week leading up to the actual Five Peaks record attempt, I was training twice a day six days a week. The sessions included working on the famous Coughlin Hill in the Phoenix Park, where Eamonn Coughlin reputedly did much of his spade work prior to his brilliant gold at the 1983 Word Championships. We also included a series of 10K and 5K runs along the way, including the 5K Jingle Bells charity race which takes place every Christmas, also in the Phoenix Park. My first one of these, undertaken in December 2003, resulted in a time of twenty-three minutes and thirty seconds – most of the racing club girls passed me along the way with considerable ease! It's quite amazing to think the week I came home from Everest, I ran a treadmill 5K nearly six minutes quicker than that...

And so, by the time the challenge approached on 25 June 2004, with all the training done, Lorcan remained the fittest, Cathal the strongest, Niall the toughest and me? Well, only time would really tell.

I was in the best shape of my life. I was fit, strong and, importantly, more determined than any laboratory test could ever measure.

I had met a girl named Catherine leading up to the challenge. It was she who taught me the essence of humility and the wisdom to see mountains as more than mere obstacles to be climbed. She made me promise that I would say a prayer asking the mountain for safe passage and offer thanks each time I came off. She gave me a jade stone, which she packed away in my platypus pack together with a small mantra which reminded me of the words echoed in the Gloria Gaynor track 'I Am What I Am'. Finally, I felt that what I was needed no more excuses. I was ready.

At 8.20 p.m. on the evening of 25 June 2004, we broke the world record for the Five Peaks Challenge by a staggering thirty-two minutes to create a new record of sixteen hours and sixteen minutes, which remains unbroken to this day.

The gods were with us for sure. The final ascent up Ben Nevis was done bare back, in punishing temperatures of 27°C heat. The tricky and speedy descent was overseen by the very generous lads from the Scottish Mountain Rescue team who led us down at incredible speed through the less travelled, and considerably more dangerous, scree slopes which I did virtually on my backside. My knees were completely shot and I screamed out in pain continually until the ground finally levelled off beyond the river below. The air speeds mountain to mountain were just right for the Augusta helicopter's travels. Our total flying time, which is included to make the record, was four hours and fifteen minutes, meaning that the actual five peaks were covered in just under twelve hours, quite an achievement for a guy who could barely climb three of them by land and sea some four years previously.

Despite serious sugar shortages on several of the mountains (I was down to my last Kellogg's Nutri-Grain bars), most especially on the decent of Scafell, where I nearly passed out, we had done it as a team. Each one of us discovered the essence of humility, the necessity of teamwork and the fulfilment of our self-esteem. No person is greater at any point in the chain than the weakest link. Interestingly, at one point or another, each of us occupied that link.

I had promised that I'd smoke a cigar that evening, but, in truth, I was barely able to eat the celebratory dinner.

The next morning we were back in Dublin. The media had been exceptionally kind to us and I will never forget the support that everyone at the ASI and Shire gave us. Incredibly, I was travelling that same day, the 26th, down to Kerry to do an outside broadcast for Radio Kerry to cover their *Sunday Gold Show*. I'll never forget having to get one of the gardaí to help me walk up to the OB (outside broadcast) unit outside Fitzgerald Stadium where Sheryl Crow was playing. I could barely walk. The weekend was capped off with my buddy Catherine Halloran from *The Star* and her friend Iona, with whom we stayed. The girls each had to help me up the stairs to get me back into bed, my legs were that badly hit.

Several more challenges followed each year, in quick succession.

We famously decided, for example, to explore Croagh Patrick in 2005. We (well, Cathal) were genuinely curious to see just how many times that mountain could be scaled in a twenty-four-hour period. We chose Croagh Patrick because you are climbing immediately on this mountain. There is immediate height gain from the off. Cathal's fastest ever up and down to the car park was an incredible fifty-eight minutes! We wanted to test the human body to the absolute limit and to see how quickly we could ascend and descend 35,000 feet. To do this, we would have to get up and down Croagh Patrick seven times.

We were joined in that summer's efforts by Michael O'Riordain, a consultant orthopaedic surgeon based in the Waterford Regional Hospital. The support we got from the people of Westport was quite incredible, most especially my then girlfriend, Catherine, and the staff of the Westport Inn, who were outstanding with food, accommodation and a memorable party when we'd finished. We raised some money too for the work of the Irish Osteoporosis Society. The grandson of Professor O'Brien, the society's founder and chairperson, joined us for the second half of the climb and once again the guys from Shire played a blinder, with Paul Kavanagh, the sales manager, even doing an ascent himself. In all, we climbed the majestic peak seven times in just over seventeen hours, giving us our 35,000 feet of pretty horrendous climbing up and down. By the seventh ascent, we had bloody feet and blisters that kept the generous nursing and physio staff of the Castlebar Hospital on their toes. Trish, Cathal's patient and understanding better half, rallied the troops from far and wide to make sure we had the support of friends and families, cheering us on to the end.

The challenge stands out in my mind for two reasons: the ice buckets that we climbed into after the fourth descent to drain the excess lactic acid, and Catherine's amazing patience with me on the final ascent. Bloodied and badly blistered, I didn't really have any right to go up the scree slopes one last time, but she encouraged me all the way. I'm really not sure I would have made it without her amazing support and kindness.

I believe it was just after the successful seventh and final descent that I announced to Cathal that I was going to try to break the world record for the Seven Summits of the World. 'That lad must have gotten two much sun up on that there mountain,' remarked one of the old lads, who overheard our conversation at the bottom.

9

Let the Games Begin

'Upon the conduct of each depends the fate of all.'
Alexander the Great

Tony was already half-drunk. Oblivious to his surroundings, the self-proclaimed 'king of scrap' was in flying form and the jokes were non-stop. Though it was also the first time in the six miserable days since we'd arrived in the world's most southerly point that Tony Jones, my witty life-saver of a climbing colleague from Wales, had managed to keep the jokes clean! It made me smile.

It was 10 January 2007 and, as I turned to look around me, aware that my thoughts were being drowned out by a bar full of Chileans who spoke little or no English, my mind began to drift back over the crazy year that had just been. I had been triple-jobbing it all year to pay the bills and complete the technical training. I recalled the many touch-and-go moments concerning John Whittle and whether or not I'd be able to get my cameraman, and now friend, over to join me and, of course, the enormous pressure and perceived jeopardy that surrounded not only me but the entire world record attempt itself.

Everything now depended on factors out of my control: the runway conditions on our pending flight to Antarctica, the unpredictable prevailing crosswinds, which had to be less than twenty-five knots at our landing site, the Patriot Hills Base, not to mention the feasibility of being able to service the giant Russian Ilyushin cargo plane, capable of transporting 165 tonnes of weight, that would eventually carry us and the 'last-degree' skiers who were bound for the desert of perpetual ice and snow.

That night, however, that flight seemed a million miles away, and we'd already been put on hourly alerts up to 7 p.m. each evening by ALE (Antarctic Logistics and Expeditions), essentially the people in charge, who were responsible for our rather complicated safe arrival and departure from the Vinson Massif, the first of the seven peaks we were to climb.

Oh well, I thought, shrugging my shoulders, *nothing else for it. Let's get bloody hammered!* I'd already had two cocktails and I could taste the salt on my lips. It was inviting. I hadn't drunk properly for almost two years, such had been the intensity and level of my training. Right now, though, as we waited for the go-ahead, I needed something to take my frustrations out on.

Memories remain very vague of what followed that night; in fact I have none at all. The next morning, I woke feeling rather the worse for wear. David Pritt had escorted me back to the hotel, the Tierra del Fuego, apparently saving me from the embarrassment of urinating in the neighbouring alleyway. Meanwhile, Tony Jones – escorted by his trusty comrade-in-arms from Yorkshire, Simon Biltcliffe, who was built like he was made out of concrete blocks, and John, our new mate from Liverpool who we simply called 'Scouser' – had led a full-scale assault on the half a dozen or so bars that surrounded Magellan's statue in the centre of the town. Perhaps even Magellan himself might have afforded the boys a smile that night. After all, there was a long and colourful history surrounding the Welsh and their connections with this region.

The part of Patagonia that lies in southern Chile contains many nineteenth-century Welsh settlements and is commonly referred to as 'Gwladfa Patagonia', or so Tony had proudly informed me. The Welsh had also started settling south and west of the foothills of the Andes and undertook a number of mining explorations in the area. It was, in fact, through these explorations that the Andes were originally settled.

No wonder the man was having such a ball; it was in his blood, while the rest of us couldn't really wait to leave!

A mixture of guilt and anxiety gripped me the next morning over breakfast after my over-indulgence. I decided to go for a walk, to try and clear my head, get some fresh air and find out where I could get some decent cardiovascular exercise.

Punta Arenas, where we were stranded, lies in Chile's southern-most region of Magallanes and Chilean Antarctica. The area means sandy point, a notation, in fact, that appeared on sailor's charts in the 1700s. The entire region has a population of no more than 125,000 people, comprising mainly those of Spanish, Yugoslav, German, French, Italian and British descent. As I had rapidly discovered, Spanish was what you needed if you hoped to prosper around here – and it was a language I didn't know.

I felt a bit of a chill as I started to walk about the strangely linear streets. Temperatures in summer here rarely rise above 18°C degrees, which made it feel, somewhat disconcertedly, like home. Though the sun, which is perched high in the southern sky, can still burn you if you don't have proper sun protection. After several hours of wandering and contemplating, I eventually found news that eased my conscience about the amount I'd drunk the previous night. 'Thank God,' I muttered. I had found out that there was a local ski hill, Cerro Mirador, which had a network of trails leading through a forest and up onto the open hilltops that overlooked the surrounding town.

For the next three days, we ran and spluttered the approximate ten kilometres up to the terro, and then took some solace in the hills surrounding it that gave us a pretty serious workout and helped to counteract the weight we were beginning to add to our bodies. Dave was the only one that remained behind. He preferred, understandably, to wait for news and deal with the various logistical issues that needed to be sorted out, such as baggage and gear allowance for our flight on Big Bird.

I had weighed myself on the first day of our exercise regime, and was alarmed to discover that I was now weighing in at eighty-seven kilos, the heaviest I'd ever been. 'Damn,' I announced to Tony, 'even your out-half for Wales Dwain Peel doesn't weigh that much, and he's five foot ten, the same as me!'

No wonder Tony was smiling back at me: standing at five foot six, the guy weighed an incredible twenty-five kilos less than I did. There wasn't a pick on him. You had to love him – he was not only funny and extremely generous, but was also a very positive individual. Somehow, life seems to get easier when you make it, and Tony had made it big time. His 'scrap' company DTC Telecoms, which he had built from scratch, began its life in Northern Ireland clearing old telecoms and cabling equipment and selling it on for scrap, and considerable profit. Even today, the company uses the services of a local prison in Wales, whose inmates separate various metals among other things. To prepare for this challenge, Tony had sensibly hired the services of a personal trainer for a number of months before we left.

Simon, who was equally bright and successful, again establishing his own company called Web Mart, was six foot but was ten kilos heavier than me, tipping the scales at around ninety-five kilos. And then there was Dave Pritt, who was ten years older than me and probably fitter at that stage, considering he'd successfully led a client expedition to the top of Vinson less than two weeks earlier. He even managed to get to play a game of football on the ice to celebrate Christmas Day.

Mind you, I needn't really have worried about my weight for, as my very patient dietician Orla Duffy had pointed out, there wasn't ever going to be enough weight on my body to counteract what I would lose when we left the base camp at Patriot Hills and started on the challenge. I still did 200 press-ups every day, much to the annoyance of John, as he lay on the bed most afternoons smoking rollies and sorting through camera footage. John was fifty-eight and not very fit.

☙☙☙

I'll never forget standing on Baggot Street beside Orla's car being weighed on the special tetra scales, which broke everything down including your percentage of body fat. It was Christmas week, just before we set off for Chile and though standing on one of Dublin's busiest streets in peak traffic might have seemed like a ludicrous place to meet, such was the level of pressure to get everything done and completed, that meeting people en route to another meeting didn't seem strange to me at the time. The sigh of relief when I stepped off the scales was noticeable on Orla's face. 'Well, Ian, congratulations! You are now officially good in my eyes to go and embark on your mad but wonderful challenge.' I had 15.8 per cent body fat. Orla wasn't happy to sign me off unless I had 16 per cent and she had managed to get me within 0.2 per cent of that. When I had finished the 100-hour Challenge six months earlier, I had had less than 10 per cent. It was quite an achievement by Orla to be fair. It's so hard to explain just how difficult it is to hold extra fat and substantially more muscle and still remain cardiovascularly and aerobically fit. Orla was desperately afraid, given the fact that I planned to boldly go to sustained altitude and recover in periods shorter than any other human being had ever done, that I might have trouble holding onto my body fat, let alone the muscle.

It may be difficult for some of you reading this not to laugh when I tell you that I struggled to put weight on and to find food that contained good fats. Looking back, it's very hard not to overemphasise just how important fat is to our daily diet. All fats are a mixture. I found it useful along the way to try and remember the adage that good fats contain small amounts of bad fat, and the bad fats contain small amounts of good fat. With the wrong fats, you eat up to six times more in order to get the right fats. Imagine, therefore, what the lads in Crunch Fitness used to think when they saw me consuming whole blocks of Charleville Cheddar after training (the only cheese I actually liked to eat in such huge amounts) and two to three 500 milligram cartons of yogurt in the late summer days of July 2006.

Back then, my weight was just under twelve stone, having completed the gruelling Ulster Bank 100-hour Challenge. Scaling every one of the twenty-six peaks of Ireland, North and South, in ninety-eight hours will knock the pounds off you in no time, let me assure you, and my diet plan was about to radically change from that point on for the next six months leading into the Seven Summits Challenge.

The issue, of course, that we all have to remember when we sit down to the table is not how much fat we consume, but rather, how much of the good fat we actually consume, and how much of the bad. The right fats are essential to our daily lives. They help to transport oxygen to every cell in our body, and they are the solid basis for every hormone, brain and nervous system function. Fats, therefore, as I came to fully appreciate eventually, are rather essential. Without them, as Orla and others reminded me, nothing works. Those guys even help to protect us from cancer. It was frightening to think that the wrong fats could in fact help to allow certain cancers in, partly because they compromise the integrity of our cell membrane. And so, thanks to the hype in the media, those of us who care enough spend our time desperately trying to avoid all those bad boys, which include trans fats, cross-linked fatty acids, double-bond shifted fatty acids, and dozens of other compounds that do not occur in nature and are simply beyond my general comprehension!

It may surprise you to know that, in the end, the cool Italian balsamic vinegar dressings that are sold in our supermarket stores did the trick nicely and allowed me to put on those necessary pounds.

Around the end of September 2006, I had headed over to the west to see Brian Hughes, an old pal of mine, who, together with his dad, Paul, ran one of Ireland's most entertaining hotel establishments, the Abbey Glen Hotel. This is one of those places that simply felt like home and the Hughes family are just about the most gracious hosts you will find anywhere. I was there, though, to do some hard-core training and anyone familiar with that part of Clifden will agree when I say that it has some of the most stunningly beautiful running routes, most especially the Sky Road run which meanders alongside the rugged coastal beauty of Connemara.

When I was there, *The Star* had asked the hotel to lay out all the food that I consumed in my 4,000-plus calories-a-day diet. Suffice to say, it took the staff several patient hours to lay it all out in its splendid glory.

☙☙☙

The food in Punta Arenas, while reasonably priced, wasn't on par with the culinary delights of home, except for the steaks, which were delicious. I didn't get to drink much of the excellent Chilean wines that were around either.

Apart from that one boozy evening, I preferred to stay about the hotel most of the evenings, and hope, like everyone else who was stranded and dotted about the town, that we'd soon be getting some news from the ALE lads. John and I generally had a good laugh together and had hit it off really well with the two lads, Tony and Simon. Anxious to get some interesting footage in the can, we decided to hire a car and head south in pursuit of humpback whales. It was a fascinating journey and prompted us to ask about taking a longer trip to the famous Torres del Paine. Declared a Biosphere Reserve by UNESCO in 1978, the Torres del Paine National Park (located in Chilean Patagonia) is internationally renowned as one of the most beautiful, unspoiled and remote places on the planet.

It was on a very frustrating Day Nine that tempers finally began to fray. Being stuck in a Chilean version of Groundhog Day was starting to take its toll on everyone. Some people were even starting to become suspicious that the delays were on purpose. But that's simply not true, as any interference with safely landing the remaining fifty-plus passengers, who represented that year's last visitors to Antarctica, would be more than costly for the ALE operators. Every flight on the Russian Ilyushin in and out of Patriot Hills cost a staggering $250,000-plus so they were, in truth, as keen as we were to send in the last of the 2007 explorers.

John joined me in the computer room after lunch, deeply frustrated. His tone was sombre. 'Ian, the money still hasn't arrived in the account. I'm afraid if it doesn't arrive this week, I won't be joining you on the trip and will head back to the UK.'

What else was there to say? Once again, I found myself trying to get through on my mobile phone to my own bank and to the investors to see what was going on. Had the bridging finance come through to my bank? John was waiting on the first part of the €60,000 fee we agreed.

I could hardly blame him for putting things to me in a straight-up fashion; he had his own commitments to keep. The financial pressures remained enormous and, despite being at the bottom of the world, they weren't going to simply disappear.

The moment that I had decided to try to make the world's first documentary of the Seven Summits Challenge, I knew I was going to need several rather large miracles to pull it all off. Now that we had been stranded in Chile for such a long period, there would be considerable accommodation and living costs to be added to the total as well. It never occurred to me that there would be serious cost issues down the line when we tried to change flights for our onward journeys. Rather naïvely, I had thought the budgets given to me by Adventure Peaks included flexible flights and, to be fair, so did my sponsors at Ulster Bank, who had been really supportive on a number of fronts.

Just convincing a bank in the first place to trust a guy who up to that point hadn't been to altitude was quite an undertaking. So often when it comes to sponsorship, it's about being in the right place at the right time. But far more significantly, in terms of the actual sponsorship coming good, it's usually defined by that area of common interest that exists between both parties – the bigger the sub-circle linking them, the better the chances of overall success.

The bank was starting to move in different directions when I first approached them in November 2005. They wanted to do something very different corporately over the coming two-year period; something that would be perceived as going against type for a bank.

Amongst other things, they had a keen interest in and mandate for supporting people who operated at the heart of the community, in various locations across the country. Denis McArdle, from the business banking section, with whom I had had a number of dealings over the years through Operation Rudolph, opened the first door. As fortune would have it, Sarah Dempsey had taken over as head of sponsorship and she and I knew each other from our old PR days. Sarah, to her eternal credit, put her faith in people to deliver concepts and always considered the bigger picture first. She was one of those positively inclined individuals and we got on very well. The agreed sponsorship of our Seven Summits Challenge, costed primarily on the budgets Dave Pritt had submitted, also generously allowed for certain pre-marketing activity in 2006, such as the 100-hour Challenge around Ireland.

My proudest association with the bank, though, came through our Fly the Flag Competition, which we had opened up for primary schools across Ireland. We had asked the kids to design the flags that I would plant at the tops of the various mountains. But far more importantly, I wanted the kids to give a message to the world under various themes, such as love, hope, family and health. I had no idea at the time just what a catalyst those flags would prove to be. Funny, isn't it, how you come to feel that you are not just doing something for yourself but holding the dreams of the next generation.

The core budget for the actual challenge naturally covered the various mountain permits, so often the stumbling block for those with Seven Summits ambitions. Vinson alone was coming in at $30,000, for example, and my basic travel and accommodation around the world was also covered. Dave's calculations, of course, were based on the minimum stopovers and, as I was soon about to discover, there was no flexibility in the flight ticket. Minimum stopover, incidentally, meant that the accommodation allowance ran out after two nights.

As if by divine intervention, day ten finally signalled an end to our woes and the hourly countdowns finally resulted in something tangible. We were leaving!

Our luggage had to be separated into four distinct categories for pre-boarding. We would have one set of clothing for our arrival on Antarctica, which included our parkas, wind pants, the mad double-layer Everest boots more suited visually for a lunar trip, goggles, gloves and sun protection. All the group gear – food and extra clothing – would go in the hold. We were allowed minimum hand luggage, for items such as passports and cameras, and all the 'city' gear and clothing would be left in the hotel till we came back. The allowed weight per person was 52 kilos in total. This might seem like a lot, I'm sure, but when you're packing for the unknown, it was an easy total to reach.

Once we cleared immigration and security, we stepped out onto the runway. After all the waiting, nothing could really prepare us for the spectacle in front of us. It was if they had merged three jumbo jets together. The Russian Ilyushin is the biggest craft I have ever seen – it is actually a four-engine, long-range, wide-body airliner and features supercritical wings fitted with winglets, a glass cockpit and a fly-by-wire control system. It was first flown in 1988 and certified in 1992.

The plane had been bought by ALE to replace the old Hercules that was first used to transport passengers. After we'd done the cursory filming, we boarded minus the air hostesses and were greeted by rather burly Russian servicemen, who didn't speak very much English and preferred to point at things instead. Our passenger seats were bolted to the floor. The rear of the plane was already packed and tied down with the enormous amount of freight we were carrying. They handed us ear muffs. Just as well too, as the noise from the engines was deafening. I felt like I was on board a flight that would be soon flashing the red lights and opening its side door in anticipation of our parachute jumps. I sat back and tried to close my eyes.

As Big Bird finally launched into the sky, bound on its four-and-a-half hour course that would take us over Cape Horn and across Drake's Passage and eventually into the very heart of Antarctica, I smiled nervously to myself, wondering what the hell I had let myself in for.

10

You Want Ice? You Got Ice!

'Each difficult moment has the potential to open my eyes and open my heart.'

Myla Kabat-Zinn

I've always felt that there is no greater fear than that of the unknown. How can there be? In our relationships, for example, is there anything more frustrating than not knowing where you stand with that other person, compounded, of course, if your feelings for them are crystal clear in your own mind?

The sense of insecurity you feel within yourself only grows with time. And though it's painful to break up, it's still easier than not knowing, the lesser of the two evils. If you are diagnosed with having a serious illness, you will find that the hardest part (if, of course, you're fortunate enough to make a full recovery) is the agonising wait for the results of your tests. 'I can deal with anything, just as long as I know what I'm dealing with,' you bravely tell yourself. Of course, there are some things – a shock or something we just didn't see coming – that we simply just can't prepare for. The trick, I guess, is learning to accept that we can only worry about the things we have actual control over. Sometimes, we just have to let go of the rest.

Despite reading up ferociously on the great expanse of snow and ice that I could see below me, nothing had prepared me for the sheer vastness, remoteness and sameness of the Antarctic. But for all of that, the mountains and glaciers that paraded theatrically below us were intensely beautiful to behold. They were also intensely white. The scene as we came in to land was reminiscent of a giant wedding cake, with the glacial intrusions serving as the figurines on top.

It surprised me to learn that the Vinson Massif, the mountain that I was about to try and climb, had not been discovered until 1955. I thought that, somehow, after the great exploits of the likes of Shackleton and Crean, that the mountain would have fallen long before that. In fact, the mountain was first spotted by chance by US navy pilots during an aerial reconnaissance mission for the American International Geophysical Year Traverse Party, to give them their full title. It was named after Carl Vinson, a United States Congressman from Georgia who was a keen supporter of research in the Antarctic region. Further aerial and ground surveys between 1958 and 1961 not only established heights for all the respective peaks but also found that there were two distinct ranges within the mountains themselves. Those to the north, including Vinson, kept their original name of Sentinel Range, while those in the southern group became known as the Heritage Range and the entire collection was named the Ellsworth Mountains. They are named after Lincoln Ellsworth, who, after completing the world's first trans-Arctic crossing in the airship *Norge*, attempted in 1935 to make the first ever transcontinental flight over Antarctica. He fell just short of the Bay of Whales, but from the plane he observed this jagged, 'solitary little range' of mountains jutting out of the landscape.

What probably surprised me even more was the fact that Vinson was a staggering 1,200 kilometres from the South Pole itself, which perhaps helps to explain why Crean *et al* didn't know about it, as they didn't get the opportunity to venture so far inland.

At the southern end of the Massif, the mountain is capped by Mount Craddock, which peaks at just over 4,650 metres. Given, the fact that this was the last of the seven continents' peaks to be climbed, it was hardly surprising that the Americans pressed hard for a first summit. Incredibly, despite their keenness to succeed, they would have to wait a further five years till that dream was finally fulfilled. In early December 1966, a ski-equipped US navy Hercules landed ten of the best American mountaineers on the Nimitz Glacier, some eighteen miles from the actual summit. Three camps were subsequently established and, on 17 December, the American team had their coveted prize, courtesy of Barry Corbert, John Evans and Pete Schoening. The boys stayed a whole forty days, during which time they bagged six peaks in total, including the four highest on the continent. The studious mountaineers among you reading this will appreciate that Tyree is the most challenging climb of the lot and stands, I was very glad to hear, just forty-five metres shy of Vinson. For those of you contemplating challenges in Antarctica, you might like to consider that Corbet and Evans remain the only partnership to have climbed the three highest peaks in the region.

Jon Krakauer in his book *Into Thin Air* suggests that there might be more kudos for climbers if they contemplated climbing the second highest summit on each continent, thereby ensuring that peaks such as K2 and Tyree were tackled. Respectfully, as I look back now, I think that challenge is for the pure technical climber.

Such exciting tales and achievements were, nevertheless, very far from my mind as I came off the Ilyushin plane, crawling through the massive back door and facing into the coldest winds I have ever encountered. We all needed extreme care stepping off, as we were surrounded by a menacing trail of blue ice. You couldn't cross safely without crampons, and just putting them on sapped your energy in this most hostile of environments.

Somehow, the plane had miraculously landed on the deadly runway of ice, despite tail winds that I found out later were in excess of thirty-five knots. Those former MIG pilots who flew in the Russian–Afghan war in the 1980s are on my Christmas list this year for the biggest and best vodka money can buy!

We were quickly guided by the base commander and his staff, following the various marker wands as best we could, towards the Patriot Hills Base Camp, which was about a mile or so ahead in visibility that stretched no further than your nose. It was blowing an almighty hooley and you could feel the wind ripping viciously through any exposed part of your skin. It was full balaclavas and face protection at the ready.

About 500 metres into the journey, I turned to find John and see if he had captured anything on film. Unbeknownst to me, my cameraman had fallen on the blue ice and later, as I would regretfully discover, had a suspected cracked rib, not the ideal form of preparation for climbing into altitude.

Conditions didn't improve as we arrived into camp, which was remarkably well kitted out with several large and well-constructed mess and cook tents and toilet facilities that comprised igloo-style sheltering with a forty gallon drum wearing a loo seat! There were a number of various two- and three-man accommodation tents dotting the horizon. As it was our first night, we were allowed into the main mess tent and even given food and wine. This was a simple courtesy and was a gesture that was not repeated. Dave felt it best, however, for us to get out and make up our tents, as he didn't want us sleeping in the mess tent. How we got the three tents up in winds surpassing 100 kilometres an hour, I'll never know and just how I avoided frostbite is beyond me. I could feel the hairs in my nostrils freezing, my hands and fingertips were piercing with pain, and my face was completely numb.

Let's hope the bloody weather improves for us on the glacier, I thought, *or else I simply won't make it without getting ripped to shreds.* That night, as I lay in my tent, with the 100 kilometre per hour winds scouring the surrounding landscapes, I thought back to that frightening day in Punta Arenas in the Serbian Climbing Club, where we had been shown graphic photographs by the attending doctor of just what can go wrong in bad weather conditions. It had completely scared me. Frostbite, as the doctor explained, is classified by actual degree of injury (first, second, third or fourth), and simply divides into two types, superficial and deep. Most frostbite injuries affect the feet or hands. But these weren't the only graphic injuries we were shown.

The remaining 10 per cent or so of cases typically involve the ears, nose, cheeks and, yes, the penis. We heard the story of a guy who went to take a leak, only for his zipper to freeze and, within a matter of twenty seconds, the damage had been done. Once frostbite sets in, the affected part begins to feel cold, and usually numb, which is followed by a general feeling of clumsiness. The skin turns white or yellowish. Many patients experience severe pain in the affected part during rewarming treatment and an intense throbbing pain that arises two or three days later and can last days or weeks. As the skin begins to thaw during treatment, edema (excess tissue fluid) often accumulates, causing severe swelling. In second- and higher-degree frostbite, blisters appear. Third-degree cases produce deep, blood-filled blisters and, during the second week, a hard black scab forms. But in fourth-degree cases, the frostbite penetrates below the skin to the muscles, tendons, nerves and bones. In such severe cases, the dead tissue will mummify and eventually drop off. As I lay there in my special down duvet, freezing and scaring myself with such gruesome thoughts, another notion occurred to me – it wasn't getting dark outside. I began to wish that I had swiped one of those eye masks from first class, on one of the earlier long-haul flights. Seven days of the 'living daylights' lay ahead. Still, I had my Sony Walkman to help drown out the sound of the wind outside. I tuned the volume to maximum and let the soothing sounds of Fleetwood Mac's *Rumours* album do the trick.

Perhaps not surprisingly, the weather didn't improve the following day. It would take another two days for the winds to drop sufficiently to allow us to board the small but remarkable twin-engine Otter that would bring us on the final hour of our journey to the foothills of the Branscomb Glacier, where the climbing would finally begin. Sometimes, you have to make the best of the situation you find yourself in and, luckily for me, there were a number of amazing people at Base Camp whom we would get to interview for the documentary. Two especially would change my outlook on life forever. I firmly believe in fate and the notion that people come into our lives for a very good reason, be it for a day, a month or a season, as the poem goes.

Sean Swarner looked more like a male model straight off the cover of a magazine. He was tall, athletically built and had a smile that could have lit the Alaskan plains. He certainly didn't look like a guy who had twice cheated death and beaten Hodgkin's Disease and Askin's

Disease, at odds of over 2 million to one. It was hard to physically detect that this man had only one lung and had become the world's first cancer survivor to climb Everest. You wouldn't have known by his demeanour that, at fourteen, he had been given two weeks to live and that a mere two years later, he would suffer an even more destructive form of lymphatic cancer. Sean Swarner made me want to be a better human being. It was all I could do not to shed tears as I interviewed him on camera, listening, ashamed at my own selfishness and 'poor me' attitude.

He said something that day that touched me very deeply as he smiled at me, placing his hand on my shoulder. 'Ian, we survive twenty days without food, a possible three days without water but, my Irish friend, you won't last thirty seconds without hope.' My artificial world of materialism and false beliefs had just been shattered forever.

Sean, like me, was climbing the Seven Summits. He wasn't in The same egotistical hurry that I was, but he'd just three to go. His book, *Keep Climbing*, was going to be launched the following month on *The Oprah Winfrey Show* and his incredible website – www.cancer climber.org – should be visited by everyone. Sean Swarner and the things he stands for – courage, humility and unflinching hope – are the reasons why I am alive today, teasing out these life-changing events in this book.

Somewhere in the middle of those two incredible days, two figures resembling Mr and Mrs Claus appeared miraculously in the main mess tent. At first, I thought I was on a movie set watching Donald Sutherland perform in a follow-up to *Miracle on 34th Street*. Not only did this man's entire features resemble those of Donald Sutherland, but he spoke like him as well. It turns out that this doppelgänger and his wife were the first American couple to walk to the South Pole.

His name was Ray Jardine and he remains one of the most inspiring figures in the history of global adventure. Ray, who was born in 1945, is an American rock climber famous for being the first to free climb the west face of El Capitan in the Yosemite Valley, and also for inventing the spring-loaded camming devices that revolutionised rock-climbing, known as 'friends'. He began his climbing career in 1963 in the Tetons, climbed in Eldorado Canyon during the 1960s, and became active in Yosemite around 1970. During the 1970s, he pioneered a number of Yosemite's harder routes, including a number graded 5.12 and most notably the first ascent of the Phoenix, accepted now as being the world's first 5.13.

But this man was so much more than the sum of his impressive parts. This amazing character, once a NASA engineer, had suffered a debilitating stroke six months prior to arriving in the Antarctic and been incapacitated on one side of his body but here's the real kicker – he taught himself to speak again, to move again, to live again. He wasn't going to allow a stroke to affect his being, his love for life and pure adventure. This extraordinary individual had planned to scale the big mountains, as he put it, 'to see if I can survive for a while at altitude'. He was going to do all of this, beginning with Vinson, a matter of one week after walking to the South Pole. Lesson number two quickly sank in immediately after we'd spoken off camera and I'd managed to drag my jaw off the floor – there are always greater feats to be admired, always people who will do more amazing things than you. Simply learn from these people, draw from their attitudes and drink from the well of positivity. Surround yourself with like-minded individuals, not people who wish to drag you down and drain you.

Arriving on the mountain glacier was such a relief. A relief to all of us sun-kissed, tired and bearded individuals, who had been stranded for many days waiting for the twin-engine Otter to be able to take off from Patriot Hills, and a relief to us that we would now finally be on our way.

We were dropped with five other climbing groups; we were collectively the last climbers who would summit Vinson for the 2007 season. I remember the weather being simply magnificent and incredibly hot upon arrival – 'Mr Blue Sky' was warmly greeting us. There wasn't a puff of wind, which was staggering. The snow was a brilliant white. How could the weather be so different in such a short space of time? Well, apart from the fact that we had just landed in a valley, Vinson is best attempted during the summer months of

November, December and January, when there is twenty-four-hour daylight. Unlike, as I would later discover, the climate of many of the world's great mountains, the Sentinel Range tends to be influenced by a generally stable air mass producing very good weather and very mild temperatures. However, as I was also about to learn, in these remote parts of the world, nothing is ever that simple. Atmospheric pressure at the Poles is actually lower than it is at other latitudes, resulting in air masses being sucked into these regions at high altitudes. As the air cools over the South Pole, it descends rapidly and rushes outward at high speed. Things can change around this place in a heartbeat and temperatures are capable of dropping below −40°C.

This was our first taste of pulling sledges and, for the most part, it was a wholly unpleasant experience for all concerned. Dave would concede in retrospect that we didn't use our sledges in the most economic fashion. I could sense tension building between Dave and John from the off. John was a fully respected and qualified international mountain guide. Dave, on the other hand, who was fitter, faster and covered the ground quicker, was not. This dichotomy of talents would eventually lead to serious trouble.

We split into two groups with myself and John taking up the rear. Those with responsibility for naming these ridges should have listened to their counterparts in Alaska and called the first two miles of undulating slopes Heartbreak Hill. We watched time and time again as the contents on our sledge came tumbling off. We were severely imbalanced in truth. There wasn't a proper load distribution between what was being carried in our ninety-plus litre sacks, and what we were struggling to tow behind us. We would learn the hard way.

Even though I had worked painstakingly in the gym on the cables to be able to pull 100 pounds with each arm, nothing could prepare me for the immeasurable factors − heat, the going underfoot and the beginning of altitude.

There is much deliberation around the effects of altitude in the Antarctic due to the lower pressure and latitude. Some believe that there is actually as much as 15 per cent in the difference from altitude at more normal latitudes, which compounds breathing difficulties on summit day. Given the fact that the highest I had been to during training was the Mont Blanc du Tacul, which stands at 4,250 metres, what would I know?

John and I finally collapsed into camp several beleaguered hours after the rest of the guys. I could tell John was really annoyed; he was struggling with a number of things – his fitness levels, his sore ribs, the poorly tied sledge and what he perceived as a lack of prior communication from Dave about how things might have been best organised from the off. Tony and the lads had already built several snow and ice shelters, including a cut-out television and matching seat carved from the surrounding blocks of ice. We had some laughs doing mock interviews for RTÉ and Welsh television. Tony then amused everyone with stories about Welsh place-names. 'Oi, Paddy, what's the longest place-name in Ireland, then?'

'Newtownmountkennedy,' I replied, rather unsure.

Tony cracked up laughing. 'Try pronouncing this,' he said in amusement. 'The longest place-name in Wales is Llan-fair-pwll-gwyn-gyll-go-ger-y-chwyrn-drobwll-llan-tysiliog-ogo-goch. What does it mean I hear you ask? The church of St Mary, in the valley of the white hazel, near the rapid whirlpool, nearby the red cave of the church of St Tysilio.' Although a bit of a mouthful, this entire village name is printed on the railway sign, making the sign one of the longest in the world.

Everyone had been equipped with the dreaded wag bags for their secondary toilet needs (more about those things later) and pee bottles, all marked so that you didn't make any fatal errors with the drinking bottles in the middle of the night. There were designated pee holes marked with wands at both camps and a fabulous toilet cut out at second camp affectionately referred to as 'God's Throne'.

Despite the serious and genuine fears concerning the changeable weather approaching the dreaded headwall, which marks the beginning of the real ascent and the point at which the sledges thankfully get left behind, the weather remained relatively calm.

Tony lost a crampon near the top of the ninety-metre headwall, which could have caused him serious problems later, but because his company branding was a very distinctive yellow, myself and John were able to spot it as we criss-crossed our way to the top of the steeper section. The final mile or so to Second Camp was taken at a rather leisurely pace. We were acutely aware of the ascending altitude. While conditions remained clear and stable, you feel your lungs filling more quickly than normal and there is a slightly different taste to the oxygen you are breathing in. The last time I noticed this sensation was on a short training run in Switzerland when we did an overnight at 3,600 metres, perched below the Bright Horn Mountain. I woke up the next morning, feeling rather the worse for wear as if someone had punched me in the head, with a severe headache that didn't clear until I had drunk a litre and half of water and taken two max-strength Ibuprofen.

When the two of us finally made it in to where the camp was to be, the others were busy setting it up. We got to it and started to build our protective ice walls, level the ground for the tents and get the ice melting in motion. It takes upwards of an hour for the ice to melt and if you're dehydrated, that's very bad news indeed. Working hard at altitude is punishing even for the initiated and everyone's heads were spinning after twenty minutes of intensive labour.

By the time the second tent was finally up, the weather had begun to deteriorate and visibility had been reduced to a matter of metres. The winds were starting to come up and there was a sudden, drastic drop in temperature. I had heard about these situations. You can't afford to get caught out here. Suddenly, we forgot about our dizzy minds and started to shovel as if our lives depended on it – which, believe me, they did! There was still one guided group to come that had left base camp a day later than everyone else. In that group were several Hungarian climbers whom I had met in the mess tent before leaving. I shuddered at the thought of those guys trying to get up the headwall in these conditions. The wind just rips mercilessly through every part of you, scouring your very soul, draining you of your last drop of energy as you fight to make a few yards of progress. The difference the weather in this region can make to what otherwise would be a relatively straightforward journey is akin to asking the Manchester United first team to play their opening Champion's League fixture with both of their legs tied – the handicap is that severe.

I got to see the devastation first hand over the next forty-eight hours as we were completely tent bound, sitting nervously wondering if this climatic onslaught would ever end. John was suffering badly in his own tent. The painkillers weren't really having the desired effect and he wasn't cooking for himself, which is never a good sign. Twice, he had to resort to using his wag bag in the tent, as did Simon and Tony.

Dave and I decided to hell with that, there was no way I was going to resort to going to the toilet in my tent. I very nearly regretted my decision. The toilet area was about thirty yards directly across from where we were pitched. As I got out of my tent and began to crawl on my hands and knees, it may as well have been thirty miles. It was the toughest crawl I have ever done. I could feel the tips of my fingers going numb and the left side of my face felt like it had been removed. The desperately cold air, which was nearing −41°C, was simply unbearable. I had everything on that I could possibly have worn, including two pairs of gloves. The over glove looked as if it had been frozen solid as icicles began to form rapidly. However, the worst was yet to come. As I pulled down my over trousers in a desperate bid to position myself over the plastic bag contained in the wag bag kit, I thought my buttocks had actually frozen solid. I panicked, thinking about the guy who had exposed himself and suffered frostbite on his penis. He had just been exposed for matter of seconds. I was going to need at least a minute. I was crying out with the pain. 'Damn. It's going to have to wait.' I pulled up my trousers, got back on my knees and began the crawl home, trying to concentrate on not putting my head up, and so avoiding the brunt of the storm to my face. To be honest with you, by the time I got back to the tent, I forgot my need to go to the toilet and fell asleep as soon as my head hit the makeshift pillow of Berghaus tops and jackets. Thank God Tony in Maguire Distribution had sponsored my Berghaus clothing.

John was desperate to try and join us for the summit attempt. We had been told by the duty manager at Base Camp that we had another forty-eight hours to reach the summit or else they would be forced to pull the plug on our expedition. It was 25 January and the massive clear-up operation to dismantle everything was already underway back at Patriot Hills. We weren't going to be able to hold up the show any longer. If we didn't summit today, it was over. The record, the challenge, the support and investment would all be going south, down the Nimitz Glacier.

Dave knew John couldn't make it and was reluctant to bring him along. Temperatures had gone back to normal (−10°C) and the winds had dropped sufficiently for us to have a serious go. Roped up, we all set off. Nobody was in the mood for talking, to be honest. The last forty hours had taken a fair toll on everyone. The initial going was fine but, within an hour, John was falling behind and reluctantly decided to turn back with Dave's obvious blessing. I was annoyed and felt that John could have made it if he was given more time; how many more times would I say that?

Everyone moved well and covered the ground with speed and efficiency. The five or so hours to the pre-summit were reasonable enough as we negotiated the various snow slopes and cornices, while avoiding the well signposted crevasse dangers.

The haul up the final rocky ridge was bloody awful. We could feel the effects of the 15 per cent deficit in atmospheric pressure and, in true Antarctic fashion, breathing became considerably slower and more concentrated. The last section involves almost doubling back on yourself to reach the summit ridge and seemed to go on for an eternity. Exhausting and trying though it was, it was not impossible.

As we approached the actual ridge, we could feel a sense of excitement building. I was surprised at how narrow and exposed the actual final ridge section, consisting of 100 metres or so of undulating rocks, is. As we stood on the final pinnacle, the temperatures assisted by the wind-chill factor had dropped remarkably. It was estimated to be −30°C or so. You couldn't take off your gloves, although Dave did for a moment, which he nearly regretted, to get the photographic evidence to support the fact that we had finally summitted.

My next task was to plant the first of the seven flags. I wondered at that very moment about how the Chileans would react to my flag planting, given that they had jurisdiction over the actual mountain as part of the governing treaty that oversaw the entire Antarctic region. Even though several climbers questioned my ethics later that day, I made no apologies for planting a flag at the bottom of the world, that had been so ably put together by the children of the Educate Together Primary School in Lusk, County Dublin. To me it was a message of hope.

The trek back to base was long and tedious, but the sheer relief was overwhelming. We had made it and the operation to break the world record was still alive. Imagine falling at the first hurdle! I shuddered to think of the consequences. Coming back to where the twin-engine Otter would bring us back to the relative safety of Patriot Hills should have been straightforward. It was anything but.

I struggled terribly coming off the headwall with the extremely heavy load on my back. Getting to the sledges proved to be extremely tiring and difficult for me. As for the journey from the First Camp back to base – that was a nightmare as we struggled to keep the sledges from falling over. In the intense heat coming off the glacier, we ran out of water, which was an awful mistake. We ate snow to sustain us. Of course snow isn't ideal, but it did at least take away the dry sensation in our mouths. There were several outbursts on the journey down and the mood in the group could best be described as volatile. I was just relieved to get on the Otter, exhausted and badly dehydrated. We were stranded for a further three days at Patriot Hills and they were the longest three days of my life. On the final day, we sat on deckchairs close to the runway landing, waiting for the Big Bird to drop out of the sky.

I did my final piece to camera and a phone interview with the *Seoige & O'Shea* show, strangely subdued and unemotional. My mood was philosophical and, inside, I was annoyed that Dave and I had been fighting over stupid inconsequential things instead of looking forward and being happy at our first achievement. To be fair to Dave, he was just so relieved to see the first part of the logistical puzzle falling into place and his thoughts remained uneasy as he knew tougher challenges lay ahead before he could relax in any way, shape or form. I remember my final words to camera vividly: 'The next mountain Aconcagua will tell the real tale. I have friends who are better and stronger than me, who have failed to get up this mountain.' My real Everest waited for me and lay just over the Chilean border. Was I ready to face my demons?

11

Don't Cry For Me, Argentina

'It's not the size of the dog in the fight, but the size of the fight in the dog.'
Archie, the 5 foot 9 inch tall winner of
American football's Heisman Trophy.

Churchill once remarked, 'It is a mistake to look too far ahead. The chain of destiny can only be grasped one link at a time.' In today's frantic world, we often seek refuge in philosophies or teachings that remind us about the importance of living in the now, the moment. I have come to believe that it is only when people come to understand the true significance of how they view the past and the impending future that they can really be happy in themselves.

As I sat smiling on the bus that took us back from the airport into our hotel in Punta Arenas, with my Walkman belting out the instrumental theme from the movie *Platoon,* I was aware of several things, apart from the fact that everyone on the bus, including myself, stank in a way that I didn't realise the human body actually could. Several weeks without showers or proper washing and the body develops a potent musk that even skunks might have a hard time accepting. Despite the long beard, matted hair and hardened sun-kissed skin, what I was acutely aware of for the first time, in a very long time, were my primary functions – my breathing, heart rate and thought patterns. It was as if I were becoming self-aware for the very first time. Things were starting to have context and meaning.

I was content, firstly, with the fact that I had passed my first test and survived in an extreme and hostile environment and climbed higher than I ever had before. When my body needed to find that extra gear, it had been there. I knew that there were financial messes gathering all around me. The hotel bills, the phone bills, the new flight arrangements were all about to manifest themselves, but I knew that I would deal with what had to be dealt with as and when I needed to, even if that was very soon. These pressures weren't going to spoil my moment of reflection. I knew that the dynamics governing the overall management of the key relationships between myself, Dave and John as a unit were, at best, unstable and that this was something that was going to be an ongoing issue for all of us. Looking back, it's hardly surprising that there would be relationship issues. There was so much intense pressure attached to this epic record attempt. There was the constant financial pressure that strains any relationship more than most things do in life. There was my poor technical climbing ability that would always be there raising its ugly head, John's fitness levels and painful ribs and Dave's own insecurities regarding the fact that John was a more qualified climber than he was, even though Dave was the expedition leader and we all had to move to the beat of his drum. I'm not sure we gave Dave enough credit for the logistical job he had to do behind the scenes. But it was up to us all to manage our differences like grown men and learn to live in this pressure cooker. Our lives, not to mention the record, depended on it.

I understood and appreciated that I had taken my first baby steps, climbed the first 15,648 feet of the 140,000 that were my goal. I had made the analogy of raising a euro from the public for every foot climbed and used this in my attempts to raise funds for the charities we had nominated.

A far greater challenge, in the form of the 7,000-metre 'Stone Sentinel', now awaited us, somewhere up the dusty roads in Argentina. But that wasn't today's battle. So from this point on, as I had now painfully learned on Vinson, it was going to have to be that way going forward, one baby step at a time, just like I used to say to people on Camaderry Hill and Croagh Patrick. Confucius was right. It wasn't about how fast, or how slow, so long as you simply never stopped along your journey.

Beards grow on guys at different speeds. In my case, anything more than a couple of days and it's messy. Two weeks of uninterrupted growth was, therefore, going to test anything Gillette had devised. I had a stash of the latest Fusion blades with me and it took two in the end. I felt like I was in the shower for an eternity, washing away the stink. Weight-wise, I had lost less than expected, no more than half a stone, which actually felt comfortable. *Orla will be pleased,* I thought to myself. Dave reckoned his weight hadn't really fluctuated at all. John, on the other hand, hadn't lost any of the excess weight he was carrying, but to be fair to him, he had come as far as he could in a severe amount of pain. I believed the workout did him the world of good in the long run – after all this was a marathon not a sprint, right?

That afternoon as John, Tony, Simon and myself sat down for a relaxing pint, the conversation became quite philosophical. You could tell that Simon was a doting father. He had set up a webcam for his daughters to link in to and speak to him and he had shot more footage on his hand-held than our entire documentary to bring home and show the family.

Similarly, Tony was relieved to speak with his own daughter. Tony and Simon were going to spend a couple of days in Miami on their way home, take in the sun and do things 'Jimmy Buffett' style, way down in Margaritaville.

'Johnny, how's your son doing then?' Tony asked in between his pints and juicy steak. You could see John's entire demeanour light up when he spoke about his 'boy'. John's son had been battling with leukaemia and was only starting to come through the other side – 2006 had been a pretty bad year for the man affectionately known in mountain circles as the Silver Fox.

John Whittle, who grew up in Worsley near the Bridgewater Canal in Manchester, tells this wonderful story of a time many years earlier during his work as an instructor, when he was based up in the Glenmore Lodge in Scotland, the national centre for ice climbing. The instructors had been out for a long day with the clients and Keith Geddis, a fellow instructor, was feeling rather proud. 'Gentlemen, I like to come in at the end of the day as fresh as a daisy.' Alan Fiffe, who was more senior as an instructor, responded, 'I like to come in at the end of the season as I began.' Smiling at both, John responded mischievously with a noticeable glint in his eye, 'Well, lads, I'd like to come in at the end of my career as I started it.' John never bragged of his many notable climbing achievements, never laboured the number of first ascents he and his climbing buddies had achieved in Patagonia, for example, in the mid-1970s or the incredible feats he achieved in the European Alps such as the first winter ascent of the north face of *les droites* in France.

Nor, indeed, did John press the point about the esteemed company that he had kept over the years. He was climbing at the height of the British climbing revolution in the early-to-mid-1970s, with guys who are now regarded as the stuff of legends – the Dougal Hastons and the Doug Scotts, the Chris Bonningtons, the Al Rouses and even the great French climber Patrick Cordier, whose famous routes included the Cordier Pillar, named in his honour, which is on the Chamonix face of the Grepon Mountain.

John and I first met in France in the summer of 2006 as part of my technical climbing instruction. John was my guide. Dave, to his credit, had suggested working with John given his achievements with the camera – not least his tireless contributions to the remarkable film *Touching the Void*. John was a likeable guy from the off, who didn't fuss and believed in taking his time, 'Why rush the inevitable?' he used to say, pulling on one of his rollies. He instilled a great deal of confidence in me and, considering I had never rock-climbed before, took me on two memorable trips in the French Alps. The first was a series of technical routes through the Cloche de Clouchetons (try pronouncing that with a Fruit Pastille in your mouth) at 10,000 feet. It was on that very descent, leaping over hundreds of feet of giant boulders, that we stopped to have a sandwich and decided simultaneously that it would be extremely rude not to make the world's first documentary of the

Seven Summits Challenge. We weren't going to allow a small thing like money stand in the way of making history.

Over the week, John taught me that, to cover ground efficiently in the big mountains, you had to have a sense of balance, and rock-climbing was an essential part of the process in terms of training your feet to move more effectively on mixed ground and terrain. The Arrête des Cosmiques, which meanders impressively upwards directly across from the summit of Mont Blanc, was another compelling day's climbing that involved a tricky sling move that I wasn't sure I'd be able to master. It's funny, though, what you manage to do when your actual life depends on it. That night, we celebrated our success with two of John's mates down at the local micro-brewery. The fact that the two owners had both broken their backs through freak skiing accidents only added to the feeling that you got that this place was, in fact, inhabited nightly by real-life heroes.

Those summer days, spent training and philosophising about life in the south of France were among the happiest I had spent in many a year. Chamonix was a place that I wanted to go back to time and time again. Though I would do another spell of training there before the year was out, I remain to this day determined to visit at least once more those quaint and beautiful surroundings.

Having now recuperated for two full days, it was time to be on our merry way again. First was the flight to Santiago in northern Chile, which was memorable for two specific things: Dave, who was paranoid about gear, wanted us to wear our Everest climbing boots onto the plane. I hadn't gotten used to wearing them in public and felt like a complete idiot wandering around the airport looking like a wannabe visitor to the moon. Then, on the plane, I sat beside Ray Jardine, who had decided to do another mountain straight away, which was remarkable. If successful at this altitude, he was going to join Vern Tejas, a brilliant and flamboyant mountain guide from Alaska who undertook the first successful solo ascent of Mount McKinley in 1988, for a crack at Everest. Vern worked for one of the big American guiding companies and held a number of impressive speed records. It turned out that Vern was also attempting to break the world record for the fastest Seven Summits and, as we were flying north, he was on his way south to Kilimanjaro to bag his second peak. Suddenly, I felt like Altringham, who had claimed a significant scalp in the first round of the FA Cup but who knew all too well that their fairytale cup run could come to an end soon. Still, *this* giant-killer had to be content with knowing that he could look no further than his next opponent, one who had been beaten less than a handful of times in the previous two months of climbing attempts.

Arriving in Santiago was akin to jumping out of a freezer and landing in a frying pan. We had left temperatures of −40°C and were now in temperatures of +30°C. The heat was absolutely stifling. From here, there was one overnight trip; a bus to the Chilean border and continuing north to Mendoza, one of Argentina's most enigmatic cities, where we would have to collect our park permits for the climb.

Just how we missed the bus for Mendoza the following day remains a mystery. But after we had, there was a call from me for more funds − the first of at least a dozen calls I'd make to Bank of Ireland credit-card services.

My first limit increase was to €5,000 − no big deal, right? This was done on the spot and with every good wish for my second climb. *Great*, I thought to myself. We began scurrying about the town for a taxi that might take us to Mendoza. God only knew what they'd charge a group of naïve, sunburned westerners, but that was a chance we would have to take.

Eventually, despite Dave's own credit card being swallowed up inexplicably by one of the Chilean banks, we found someone mad enough to take us all the way to Mendoza. It was a hell of a long journey, but the driver's van had air conditioning. En route, we did several radio interviews for the stations back home and floods of goodwill messages came back. Among those who had been good enough to get in touch and send a donation was Dr Ciara Scott, a very talented English dentist who now lived in Dublin and who was just back from sailing off the Antarctic herself. She would become a very important person in my challenge as time went on.

My Sony Walkman, with the 300 songs I'd loaded onto it, was becoming more and more an integral part of my mental preparation. There were songs that inspired and, more importantly, songs that helped me focus on my breathing and the job in hand. People sometimes don't realise the power of music in terms of inspiring someone. I remember talking to Pat Fox on Tipp FM about the glorious Tipperary All-Ireland hurling success in 1987. Pat recalled how the team anthem on the bus to the matches had become Tears for Fear's 'Everybody Wants to Rule the World' – a great song that, despite being about war and a desire for power, gave the listener that all-important feel-good factor!

The other noticeable difference, apart from the influence that music was starting to have on my journey, was the volume of water I was drinking – two to three litres every day off the mountain, four to five on it. Water nourishes the body's cells and enables oxygen to be transported. I guess when you consider the fact that we secrete and lose almost nine litres day, replenishing water is vital. When you finally get into the habit of drinking it, you are slow to go back to coffee and tea, which are diuretics in any case. When you climb at altitude, you lose copious amounts of water through breathing and sweating, and dehydration is the big issue. That's why the higher you go, the more likely you are to see more yellow, even orange-like, urine deposited in the snow.

Apart from the altitude, the biggest single difference that we would face on Aconcagua, in physical terms, would be the weights on our backs. We were going to have much fuller loads to carry above the main base camp at 4,000 metres. More tents, more gear and considerably more of the horrible dry-pack altitude food we had to eat.

It's difficult to put the importance of nutrition at altitude into some kind of viable context for anyone who hasn't been to these heights. It took me many months before I left to get my own head around it. After all, here I was, about to spend more time sustained at altitude than anyone else with the shortest-ever periods of recovery. We had to get the food balance right and, to be fair to Dave and all concerned, a lot of effort had gone into ensuring that we did get it right.

The evidence for the impact of a balanced diet on actual physical performance is well documented and no one would argue with it. Little things are so important. When do you train? You always get better results in the morning, for example. How do you hydrate? Before, during and after exercise. What carbs do you take? All these things affect your performance levels. But eating the right diet can, and does, enhance your mental performance, which probably helps to explain why concentration levels aren't what they should be when you train in the evenings and why you feel so tired.

The main brain fuel is glucose, and adequate mental performance depends upon our capacity to maintain a status quo where blood/glucose levels are concerned. As the levels fall, the cognitive functions become impaired, affecting attention, vigilance and memory, which could cost you your life crossing on a big mountain. Ever slipped or lost your balance training in the evenings? The carbohydrates that you consume have a direct impact on your blood glucose levels.

As we climb higher into thinner air, we need more energy. We are taking about anything in the range of 5,000–7,000 calories per day, with even greater emphasis placed on our carbohydrate intake, which is usually a minimum of 65 per cent of the total calorific intake. Declining oxygen levels make carbs a more efficient fuel source than either protein or fat. The body fails to break down protein above certain heights, usually from 5,500 metres upwards, and altitude also affects our tastes for certain foods and lessens our want for food generally, so getting it right in the food department is essential. To that effect, Orla Duffy, my dietician, had gone to amazing lengths with Adventure Peaks to ensure that my diet plan was balanced and that I had sufficient energy drinks and bars to supplement my needs. The people behind Maximuscle, the supplement that I had been taking in training, were excellent too, with their own dietician working hard to supply me with the right kind of recovery bars and additional fluid supports. Of course, the overall goal of sustained energy provision without any loss of body mass or lean tissue was impossible because, in simple terms, climbing demands a surplus energy supply at the critically important times on a mountain, summit days being a prime example. It's during those horrible last hours of climbing that the body uses reserves for fuel, but not the glycogen and fat reserves; instead, it draws down on the body's protein supplies.

✿✿✿

It's difficult to describe the sheer beauty of the Andes Mountains. I got my first glimpse of the vast ranges on the approach to the Chilean border, which seemed to take an age to cross. They are extremely strict about documentation on both sides of the border and it's a long and tedious process to get through. The remaining 100 kilometres or so to Mendoza were lit up by spectacular electrical storms − brilliant fork lightning punctuated our night sky as we approached the wonder that is Mendoza.

You could sense that there was something very special about this place as soon as you arrived on the outskirts; it had an atmosphere that was unlike anything that I had ever sampled anywhere in the world. Row upon row of canopied restaurants peppered with people enjoying themselves sitting outside with a bottle of wine, enjoying life as it is meant to be enjoyed. The province has a total area of 148,827 square kilometres, framed by arid plains to the east and the Andes Cordillera to the west. The rivers, originating in the thaw of the Andes summits, are channelled through irrigation canals and dams. This has created three long pockets of land: the north, the valley of Uco and the south, where 85 per cent of the total population is concentrated.

Mendoza sits to the far west of Argentina and is actually closer to Santiago, the capital of Chile, than it is to Buenos Aires. The area is famous for a number of things: cheap but wonderful food, most notably the best fillet steaks in the world, superb weather and, not least, the finest wines you will find anywhere.

The area is very sunny and dry, which improves the colour of the grapes, and the relative humidity is low, but it is also relatively cool. Most vineyards are at altitudes above 2,800 feet, where the grapes grow in very beneficial conditions, with little rot and few insects or diseases, and where the wines manage to attain complex flavours, thanks to a longer growing season. One of the things that fascinated

The man who cracked Ian up in the Antarctic, Welshman Tony Jones. The boys share a joke about never exposing your thumbs at −40°C!

30 January 2007: Ian and other climbers sitting at the ice runway waiting for the Big Bird to land in the Antarctic.

At the top of the world, Everest summit, 16 May 2007. Ian, proudly
wearing his London Irish jacket, with his Sherpa Tundu.

High Camp on Denali Mountain, 25 June 2007. The team awaits a
break in the weather before pushing on for the summit. Mount Foraker
looms majestically in the distance.

29 June 2007: Bad weather greets the team as they approach the summit ridge on Denali.

30 June 2007: Finally it's over! McKeever and Pritt celebrate an incredible moment on Denali summit.

11 July 2007: Ian stands tall and proud after becoming the first person to hold world records for both versions of the Seven Summits Challenge. He is pictured wearing his Black Tie tuxedo at the top of Snowy Mount in −20°C winds.

Ian relaxing with buddy Cathal after his return home.

What a moment... Ian's godson Seany (aged 9) reaches the summit of Carrauntohill Mountain on 31 August 2007. Sean wants to join Ian on Kilimanjaro next year – watch this space, folks!

Wearing his radio hat. Ian pictured on air at 106.8 FM Country Mix studio in October 2007.

11 July 2007: The team that prepared to take on Denali. Among
those pictured is Lei from China. She was the only woman in
the team and hoped to become the first woman to complete
the Seven Summits challenge.

Ian joins his godson, Sean, at the top of Carrauntohill.

Ian joins the ladies and gentlemen of the new Ritz Carlton Hotel in Powerscourt, County Wicklow, for a fun trip up the Sugarloaf in support of the Wicklow People in Need, October 2007.

June 2004: The team prepare to board the chopper for the second leg of their Shire Five Peaks world record attempt.

Size matters! Ian pictured with Kieran Collins and the newly crowned Mr Ireland, Dave Fox. Dave went on to come second in the Mr World and Mr Universe competitions.

30 June 2007: Standing tall at the top of Denali. Ian McKeever finally smashes the world record for the Seven Summits Challenge in a time of 155 days, breaking Daniel Griffith's old record by an amazing 32 days.

me about the region was the level of foreign investment that had gone into the general area itself and particularly into wine making. Winemakers from many countries, including Jacques Lurton, and Moët & Chandon from France, have bought up tracts of land to plant with vines, and winemakers are jostling to get into Mendoza, to the city that lives and breathes wine, producing 1.2 billion litres a year. Mendoza's enormous potential is now being realised and, in the past five years, the region has built the newest and most futuristic wineries. Nearly 90 per cent of the total production of fine wine produced in Argentina is located in this area.

That night, the three of us forgot our woes, our differences and our fears, and sat down to eat at about midnight, enjoying one of the finest meals I have ever tasted. The warm air filled the night and the fine wine was drunk ever so slowly.

The following day, we met up with Ray in the city and did some filming to camera. The afternoon was taken up with last-minute purchases and sorting the paperwork for the park entry visas. I knew I was about to face my greatest-ever physical challenge. I was conscious that better climbers, indeed friends of mine who were stronger and fitter, had failed on this great mountain, Aconcagua. Nevertheless, this mountain was made for me. It would come down to a battle of physical and mental will.

I checked my belongings to make sure that I had my letters. Seven letters for the seven mountains which would each be opened the night before summit day, sources of inspiration if you will; each one provided by friends and mentors whose inspiring words would help to bring me home.

The following morning, as we prepared to leave Mendoza bound for the great journey ahead, my thoughts turned to loved ones and to going home for the first time in what would be almost two months for six days of recovery. Far away fields are always greener – the cliché is always there to remind you that you never quite manage to appreciate what you have until it's out of sight. The thoughts filling my head of seeing those I really loved were going to bring me home safe and on track. 'They will Ian, they will.' *They'd bloody better,* I thought.

12

You Don't Have to Climb a Mountain to Conquer Your Own Everest!

'The minute you start talking about what you are going to do if you lose, you have lost.'

George Shultz

'What am I looking at? What am I looking with? What am I looking for?' These were the first questions Dr Shane Murnaghan asked me the night I met him. We were out socially and I was introduced to him because he was a cousin of a cousin of mine, named Michael. I had heard Michael refer on a few occasions to some guy called Shane as the 'Ginger Ninja'. I thought it was some kind of joke attributed to the fact that he had red hair. The guy was smoking a cigar and was pretty big and reasonably broad, but he certainly didn't give the immediate impression that a balaclava and some black clothing would suddenly transform him into Ireland's answer to Bruce Lee.

My first lesson about judging someone by their appearance was learned very quickly. At the time, 2004, I was preparing to go back for the Five Peaks Challenge and thought I knew it all. What could some Ginger Ninja possibly teach me at this point? I'd moved to Wicklow, was training furiously, and was in excellent shape. What more was there, right? Of course, as I sat there talking to him, I had no idea how this guy was able to read me like a book and had all of my physical and mental vulnerabilities marked within moments. Not that he embarrassed me either. He smiled at the end of our conversation and turned to me, remarking, 'Ian, if you count yourself among the living then you are more than qualified to become a patient of mine. I'd be happy to work with you and help you to really prepare and learn to focus for what really lies ahead in your life.' Pretty profound! Despite my arrogance at the time, I am, thankfully, a curious person by nature and made an appointment to see Shane in his clinic, which at the time was located just off Baggot Street, near the Pepper Canister Church. Those appointments saved my life.

Growing up, Shane believed, like most of us I guess, that if we were really, really honest with ourselves, the world simply didn't have enough superheroes. It was something we both had in common. Personally, I was always a fan of the Marvel comics and loved to read Stan Lee's comics every week while most of the lads were reading *The Dandy*, *The Beano* or *Shoot* magazine for all the latest soccer gossip. The only comic hero that has been brought to the big screen with any kind of real authenticity for me was the original Superman played by Christopher Reeve, although I give Toby Maguire real street cred for his very human portrayal of Peter Parker, aka Spider-Man. He grappled desperately in his head, as anyone would have, with the notion that with 'great power comes great responsibility'. It may have taken Shane a little longer than Peter Parker, but he certainly came to terms with his gifts in the end. Shane was determined when he was younger to find a way to become like his superhero, Bruce Lee, whose 'nuclear charisma' was epitomised for Shane in the way that small man moved. Shane's first dabbling with the martial arts came through kendo, which promotes discipline and respect for your opponent, but also has the added attraction of an elaborate costume – you get to dress up like a superhero.

'Kendo is the ultimate discipline and you achieve the respect not to mention the whole costume thing!' Shane would always laugh as he told that story of how he got be a superhero in armour – the kendo armour, comprising a silver grilled helmet that hid your face and gave you that menacing look akin to Darth Vader. You had your chest armour, a sword called a *shinai*, and the split skirt called the *hakama*. Kendo is very physical and you generate tremendous explosive power though your deliberate movements. The art of kendo is primarily a martial arts sport, of course, due to the limitations involved in carrying a sword in public! *Kendoka*, kendo practitioners, use the *shinai* as their weapon of choice. Of course, since a metal sword is not a very healthy option in training or competition, a bamboo sword is used instead.

Steve, a friend of Shane's, introduced him to the world of *ninjitsu*. He invited Shane to join him in the new *dójó*, or training hall, that he was about to open. The ninja's reputation is put into a better perspective when some facts are brought to light. First, ninja were not wizards or witches, of course, but ordinary men and women with a unique and often misunderstood philosophical viewpoint. This philosophy became a very important part of their combat method. Hence, they refer to their art as *ninpo*, the po suggesting 'a higher order' or 'encompassing philosophy'. The samurai approach to combat was called *bushidó*; it evolved from a general set of guidelines for the gentleman warrior into a formal discipline. The ninja philosophy, though sharing many of the same values as the original samurai, evolved along a different cultural path. It was just one of the many skill sets that Shane would be able to bring to bear down the line. He went to Japan and became a black belt under the supervision of the world's greatest living exponent of the shadow warrior, Soke Masaaki Hatsumi, who is the grand master of grand masters.

There, he had his epiphany. He changed on every level – spiritually, physically and mentally. He knew how to break bones but now wanted to heal them. Shane explained to me the value of the *ninjitsu* way. The value is captured best, he said, in their powerful symbol of the sword over the heart; knowing when to be heartfelt over knowing when to fight. An important lesson to learn, the ability to consider first, consider again and only then act.

Shane's grand master in Japan was also a grand master in the Japanese treatment form known as *amatsu*, which is less diagnostic focused and more therapeutic in nature than its Chinese counterpart. The skills Shane acquired through this form simply complemented his existing knowledge base. His thirst for greater knowledge was immense. He honed his skill painstakingly in the art and practice of Chinese medicine over many years of dedication, learning and qualifications, which included being awarded a doctorate for his contribution to, practice of and pursuit of excellence in this great discipline. I've worked with many great doctors and consultants in my life, as both a PR practitioner in the area of mental health matters and through other work in pharmaceuticals, but I know no one with the breadth of knowledge that this man has about the human body and its relationship to the emotions we feel and sense every day.

Shane helped to rescue me from my opinion of myself based on the things I thought I was throughout my life. He helped me over the years to eradicate self-sabotage, not to overtrain for example, to ultimately forgive myself and in the end to learn to love myself. To start each morning by polishing my heart and giving thanks to the world in which I live, was part of the learning. He helped to raise my spirit and, for this, I will be forever grateful. He revealed to me what was possible in true spirit, in physical body and in focused mind. Through a series of methods and techniques, including the traditional forms of Chinese treatments, he helped to regulate and harmonise the flow of energy in my body. He taught me that if I left fear, grief and anger unchecked, they could kill me, if left in disharmony.

Shane used to ask me simple questions which made actual sense. 'When was the last time you ever fought with someone eating ice cream, Ian?' *Good point,* I thought. The answer was never. Here's a simple exercise to try when reading this. Ask yourself the good things that you remember about your day in thirty seconds. Now do the same for the so-called bad things. Which list wins out? I came to painfully learn and finally understand the stranglehold that unhealthy emotions have on our physical structure. When people say we make ourselves unwell and things like *'She'll worry herself to death',* they are ultimately right. So how does Shane help ordinary people like you and me? He treats the person not the disease. He recognises that the person is the aspect that creates the wellness! Just remember everyone is going to die, a certainty, but only some of us truly live.

I couldn't have prepared to face my demons and climb the Everest that awaited me in Argentina were it not for the wisdom this man passed on to me.

We had decided to ascend the 'Stone Sentinel', by the second most popular trekking route, through the beautiful Vacos Valley, also known as the Polish Glacier Route. We would descend the mighty Aconcagua the same way rather than by the busier normal route, known as the Horcones Valley Route.

We had decided to use the longer Vacos Valley Route for our ascent for various reasons. It is physically harder, a little longer (twelve kilometres, which makes a real difference on Summit Day), and would therefore continue to aid our overall acclimatisation. It is much quieter too, with only something like one in four of all climbers on the mountain taking this route and, besides all of which, there was the superior countryside, vistas, greenery, flora and fauna, all integral elements for the documentary and excellent visual accompaniment for John to work with on his Sony HD camera.

Weather-wise on Aconcagua, the word to use is unpredictable, at best! The peak itself has its own special kind of microclimate. The weather can be a pleasant 30°C in the central Andes whilst a storm is raging up on Aconcagua, with wind chill of −30°C! And during the summer months, it can be windy all of the time. In the valleys it can be 27°C, as we were about to find out, and as low as 3°C at night. At Camp 3 in the night it can be −15°C to −30°C. In the middle of the day on the summit, the temperature could range anything from −25°C to +15°C, making it essential that you get off the thing by 1 p.m., just like Everest. The daily pattern tends to be an early clearing of cloud that often provides clear weather until midday. In the early afternoon, clouds usually appear, engulfing the summit by mid-to-late afternoon, as those unfortunate enough be stranded there discover, then clearing again as night falls.

In mountaineering terms, Aconcagua is 'technically' an easy mountain if approached from the north, via either of the so-called normal routes. The Polish Glacier Route approaches the mountain, once you have left the Vacos Valley, and ascends to the base of the Polish Glacier and then crosses to the Normal Route for the final ascent to the summit.

The routes to the peak from the south and southwest ridges are the most demanding and the south-face climb is considered very difficult indeed. However, let's get a few things into perspective, shall we?

The fact that only six people had summited on the Vacos Route during the months of November and December didn't bode well for a man in a hurry! Not least, one hoping to break a world record for the Seven Summits Challenge. This mountain was going to demand superior levels of mental and physical fitness. We were about to go up the highest trail mountain in the world. The effects of altitude are severe and at the summit atmospheric pressure is 40 per cent of what it is at sea level. They say that the use of supplemental oxygen is not normally required below 8,100 metres. What I was about to witness in the coming eleven days; or so, however, would make me completely rethink that very broad sweeping statement. I was hoping to get up and down this mountain in eleven days that's half the normal time for an expedition. Dave would have considered doing it much quicker again if John wasn't climbing with us. Such consideration was obviously not a reality but once you go above Base Camp (Plaza Argentina) at 4,200 metres, absolutely nothing is easy.

We had no intention of caching our loads, in other words, doing higher climbs to build our red blood cell supply and then descending again to sleep overnight, but instead climbed in intervals of 1,000 metres each day till we summited, which is far from the norm, I can assure you! To boot, Pat Falvey, such a respected and far better climber than me, who had, to be fair, set the bar for us all to follow by becoming the first man from the Republic of Ireland to scale Everest in 1993, hadn't managed to get up this very mountain with his clients in January due to appalling weather conditions. What chance for me, eh?

Then there was the small matter of rising costs. To get the camera gear up the mountain, including the tripod, would mean extra help from Base Camp to allow John to film and extra mules in the first four days to bring that gear to Plaza Argentina. The fact that we were up against the clock didn't help matters either. But for all of that reality checking, my spirits were extremely good and I was focused for whatever lay ahead, or so I thought.

It all certainly began very well. The valley approach, though long (48 kilometres to Base Camp) and tedious underfoot, and more akin to Patrick Kavanagh's stony grey soil of Monaghan, was nevertheless bathed in warm sunshine, helping to lift spirits generally. The further up the valley we went, leaving the river behind us, the hotter it became. The terrain resembled Death Valley at times – arid, baking-hot ground which shimmered under the vicious midday sun that shone down cruelly on those who were brave enough to endure it. We were roasting alive in the heat and consuming copious amounts of fluids. I tried desperately to remain as disciplined as I could. Each morning, I would prehydrate with my Viper drinks from Maximuscle which were excellent for replacing the lost salts and electrolytes that felt like they were evaporating from my very pores. Getting at least one litre of liquid into you before you start each day is the prerequisite to any chance of success. The valley, despite its testing climate and tough, punishing conditions underfoot, was an inspiring environment.

We were joined, once again, by the legendary Ray Jardine, who was now thoroughly enjoying his rollercoaster journey, since summiting Vinson and becoming part of the first American couple to reach the South Pole. Ray was sixty-two years of age, and it felt to me as if this man's thirst for life and adventure had suddenly been reborn and you got the sense that he truly appreciated this second chance… I felt like I truly was walking in the presence of greatness. It was humbling.

Apart from the usual nasal problems that I suffered with (I was secreting a litre of mucus per day – gross, eh!), I was moving well and felt good inside. Not even the boil-in-the-bag food could dampen my spirits. Day Three saw us finally arrive at Plaza Argentina, having negotiated our treks from the Pampa de Lenas, which was at 2,700 metres, and Casa Piedra at 3,200 metres.

Plaza Argentina at 4,200 metres is a strange 'commune' to finally arrive in. Tent city would be a polite way of putting it, but prettier and less populated, they assure me, than the very different visual spectacle on the other side. The more renowned and more favoured camp (most Irish choose that route) is at the Camp de Mules, where the world's highest hotel greets you; yes, I kid you not! The route itself is some twelve kilometres shorter in total and about one and a half hours shorter on summit day. But apart from spectacular views, one other thing the Vacos Valley offered its visitors is an encounter with 'Dr Death'; well, that's what we all decided to nickname him.

You didn't get to progress up the mountains unless you passed the medical. The key criteria were blood pressure and oxygen saturation levels in the blood. John, my talisman, cameraman and all-round good guy, was still recovering from two cracked ribs and it was his turn to get his medical check-up in the little tent area. 'I am very concerned, John. Your blood pressure is 180 over 110 – critical. I'm putting you on beta blockers and we'll take it from there.' Ashen-faced, John took the news rather well, I thought. What choice did he have? He'd just quit smoking and his lungs were surely feeling it. That night was spent in song with a bunch of Welshmen, who had just come back from the summit, some successful, some not, and their brilliant guide David, whose path would cross ours again.

Either way, as far as Dave Pritt was concerned, we had to go the next morning with or without John. I said several decades of the rosary and touched the immaculate medal around my neck on more than one occasion. Acclimatisation was thankfully, despite John's rather worrying blood pressure, assured to that point at least for all three of us, coming straight from the Antarctic. Our oxygen saturation levels were all fine too, all plus 94 per cent.

And so at seven the next morning, we set off for Camp 1 with full loads on our backs, of about twenty kilos per man. A porter would take up additional group gear including extra camera equipment. Usually, most people cache as I mentioned earlier – bringing their gear up and descending back down based on the principal of sleeping low/climbing high. As we were 'speed' ascending and under severe time pressure, we wouldn't be affording ourselves such luxuries.

My music was becoming more and more important to me as I knew that that day, I would be entering a whole new reality for me just above 5,000 metres. U2's 'Unforgettable Fire' lit my path ahead.

Despite feeling under the weather, John climbed with us and successfully made it to Camp 1 at 5,000 metres. He wanted a break but to his eternal credit, twenty-four hours later, we were on our way to Camp 2, located at 6,000 metres, our final pit stop before summit day. Boy do you feel it on steep ground when you are climbing above 5,000 metres. Every step hurt. This was uncharted territory for me – Vinson Massif remained my highest peak to date, standing at 4,900 metres. I keep thinking about what Prof (Professor Moira O'Brien) had said to me, 'Ian, your haemoglobin is over seventeen. Stay properly hydrated and you'll be fine. If you don't, you run the serious risk of edema.' *Christ*, I thought, *no wonder they could never get any blood out of me, it's thicker than soup!*

Still, I was drinking between four and five litres daily. When you climb high, it's all about the prehydration. I was drinking two litres every morning and it was helping me. The higher I was going, the better I was starting to perform. Dave and I had a bad fight about John on the way to 6,000 metres. Dave felt that John's progress was far too laboured and far too slow. We eventually made it up with tears in our eyes when we set up the camp in horrible, freezing conditions. I have never in my life been as prepared mentally for what was to come. That night, I visualised stepping on to the summit. I was calm inside.

Four o'clock came and it was time to brew up. We began the tricky traverse at 5 a.m. *Whatever happens, Ian – stay focused – clear your head,* I reminded myself. I was out of the traps like a veritable greyhound, like a man possessed. I was across the traverse in an incredible ninety minutes. I was joined at the crossing point (where you join the Normal Route) by a Polish climber. He was one of ten attempting the summit. Their leader was the first guy to do a winter ascent of the north face of Everest, no less. Dave joined me shortly afterwards, minus John and minus the camera. I said nothing and asked no questions. I was perched on a ledge at the time enjoying a Maximuscle bar and some isotonic drink. On we went. Three more hours to the summit. It was now freezing cold despite the sun's welcome appearance. The trouble, of course, only really begins on the famous Canaletto, the long ascent ridge normally scree-covered and deprived of snow and ice. There's a famous boulder at 1,980 metres where people traditionally turn back, through exhaustion, weather or altitude.

At this point, I thought of Eamonn Sweetman and his misfortune at not being able to continue. We were blessed here, the weather was holding up, just! *Come on, Ian, one last supreme effort.* I kept reciting my mantra, 'I am what I am and what I am needs no excuses.'

With sixty-one metres to go, the weather turned nasty. Thick clouds were swirling menacingly off the summit head. *Come on, Ian, dig. Five minutes to get yourself up or we turn around.* I was practically on my hands and knees at this point. I was exhausted, spent. Dave, who had struggled on the Canaletto approach, turned to face me, twenty or so metres ahead of me. *Damn,* I thought painfully, I knew I'd set off too quickly. My body was empty. 'Come on, Ian. You have a flag to plant on the top. You let those kids down, those charities, those investors, your sponsors, Ulster Bank, Berghaus and Maximuscle who had the faith in you and you let yourself down. Now move your scrawny pathetic ass!' I was talking aloud at this point. This was a very personal mission and I was damned if I was going to let a bunch of six-year-olds down, never mind my other stakeholders. I'd let myself down enough times… Not today. With my last effort, I crawled onto the summit, clutching my immaculate medal around my neck. When I managed to get to the famous cross, I fell down onto my hands and knees and wept. I embraced Dave. He was generous in his praise. He knew just how much it had taken and, moreover, just how much this meant to me. I never felt prouder in my entire life. No matter what happened from this point out, I had achieved what I had always asked of myself – a supremely honest effort in body and mind.

Only three of the ten Polish climbers made it. I knew just how lucky I'd been. Approaching Base Camp on the return traverse, no more than 300 metres from camp as the crow flies, I fell down the ice slopes. My right crampon had come off (damn straps were too short to begin with – my own fault). I saw everything flash before my eyes, three seconds, then four, then bang. A rock broke my fall. Deirdre McCormack, a wise and dear friend, would have been relieved to know I was wearing my St Christopher medal. Remarkably, apart from a few bruises, I was fine, nothing was broken!

When we finally reached Base Camp, it was 13 February, my birthday. 'Let's run it out, shall we, Ian?' Dave had that look in his eye as he spoke... So we did. We arrived at the roadside eleven hours later, tired, sunburned but oh so damned proud. Aconcagua had been taken out in ten days, half the normal time. The past forty-eight kilometres had been run out in tough and seething conditions in just over ten hours. Game on! I was finally starting to believe in myself, like never before.

I was tapping into those hidden reserves that I didn't even know I had. The reserves that certain individuals like Shane and others had said were there. My outlook on life was beginning to change too. Meeting guys who have survived cancer, Everest and strokes kind of does that to you, not to mention nearly killing yourself.

At last, a sense of real perspective had enveloped me. 'Life is bloody short!' I acknowledged. Regret only the things you don't do, not the things you do. Whatever else was going to happen, I was going to make sure that my personal life was in order before 2 April, the date we'd leave Ireland for the final time bound for Everest, assuming we got that far, of course.

13

Out of Africa

*'Do not go where the path may lead, go instead where there is no path and
leave a trail.'*

Ralph Waldo Emerson

I was never a great timekeeper – let's face it! Standing at the Aer Lingus
check-in desk at Dublin Airport, with one hour and ten minutes to go
to my Heathrow flight on Sunday, 25 February, however, I felt pretty
safe that I wasn't going to have any problems with the travel plans for
the third leg of my Seven Summits journey.

'Sorry, sir, we've closed the gate. You should have been here with
two hours to spare. It's a rugby weekend.' *No kidding,* I thought. I was
one of those who had watched history unfold the previous day at
Croke Park. I'd been queuing for thirty minutes to check in one lousy
bag. 'Sorry, Ann' (as I strained desperately to see her name tag), 'this
isn't an ordinary flight for me. Miss this and I could jeopardise my
world record attempt.' Sparing everyone's blushes even further, most
of all mine before I said something really stupid, the supervisor was
called.

The 4.30 p.m. flight arrived in Heathrow at 5.50 p.m. What should
have taken fifty-five minutes in the end took one hour and twenty
minutes, following hold-ups on the Heathrow approach. Despite
everyone's best efforts, including the staff of Kenya Airlines and a
lovely air hostess on my Aer Lingus flight, I simply wasn't going to

make the 7 p.m. departure to Nairobi, which would then have allowed me to change over for the short internal skip and a hop flight to Kilimanjaro International Airport. Another night in London beckoned. Plenty of time to catch up on work. *Oh well,* I thought, *the glass is always half full, Ian.*

I'd never flown Kenya Airlines before. Boy, they're good. Gracious, kind and always pleasant and cheerful, the pièce de résistance was the movie choice. You could watch from a selection of lots of movies. You simply chose the films and then you watch them – cool, eh!

The small price I would have to pay for missing my flight would be an immediate climbing start. Once again, to be fair, we were on tight deadlines and had five days to make this particular ascent.

If you do only one climb in your entire life, make it Kilimanjaro, standing majestically at just below 6,000 metres. This is a truly amazing experience that will change the way you see things – honestly, it's that good. From the way the 120 tribes of Tanzania (the Chagga being the largest) assimilate and come together bound by no more than one common language, Swahili, to the manner in which you are treated on the actual mountain by porters, guides one and all, this is truly something to behold. The Chagga are a Bantu-speaking indigenous African tribe and the third-largest ethnic group in Tanzania. They live on the southern and eastern slopes of Mount Kilimanjaro and Mount Meru, the mountain that many sensibly chose to acclimatise on before attempting Kili. Their relative wealth comes not only from the favourable climate of the area, but also from successful agricultural methods which include extensive irrigation systems and continuous fertilisation practised for thousands of years; also they became the main tribe to provide porter and eventually guiding services on the mountain. They were one of the first tribes in the area to convert to Christianity. This might have given them an economic 'advantage' over other ethnic groups, as they had better access to education and health care as Christians.

Stepping off the plane at Kilimanjaro International Airport, it is difficult not to appreciate the special environment you find yourself in.

I would have only an hour to get to the accommodation that Dave had organised and change my clothing before setting off to join the lads. John was already there with his girlfriend, Anne. They had come out early to enable John to do some filming in peace and quiet – or so he had hoped at the time.

Kilimanjaro with its three volcanic cones, Kibo, Mawenzi and Shira, is an inactive stratovolcano in northeastern Tanzania. Although it does not have the highest elevation, Kilimanjaro is the tallest free-standing mountain rise in the world, rising 4,600 metres (15,100 feet) from its base, and includes the highest peak in Africa at 5,895 metres (19,340 feet), providing a dramatic view from the surrounding plains. It lies 280 kilometres from the Indian Ocean and just over 400 kilometres from the stunning Lake Victoria. It sits on the eastern side of the eastern branch of what is known as the Great Rift Valley, and north-northeast of the Masai Steppe, the great plain of northeastern Tanzania renowned as the homeland of the world-famous, nomadic Masai cattle-herders.

Principal human habitation lies on the southern and eastern slopes of Kilimanjaro, where the fertile and well-watered soil supports farming, especially horticultural crops produced by the Chagga people. The city of Moshi, which we had passed though on the way, lies just over thirty kilometres from the summit, and, not surprisingly, is the main urban centre. From there, the paved highway and rail connections link the Tanzanian coast to places like Tanga and the country's capital city, Dar es Salaam. There's even a nightclub in Moshi, this small shanty town that throbs daily with life! If you really want to know what it is to be happy without material wealth, come and meet these people. It's a very humbling and rewarding experience, a real kick to the egotistical and superficial world of materialism, a sort of wake-up call to those whose lives are consumed with keeping up with the Joneses.

The area's tourist industry is served by the rather quaint Kilimanjaro International Airport. Culturally, this mountain has touched so many of our lives, even those who may never climb it. Mount Kilimanjaro was the inspiration, of course, and backdrop for Ernest Hemingway's classic short story 'The Snows of Kilimanjaro', which he wrote back in 1936. He also wrote a non-fiction account of his safari experiences in the 1950s, posthumously published as *Under Kilimanjaro* – it is worth reading too! The mountain is referred to, as all die-hard fans will know, in one of those brilliant *Monty Python's Flying Circus* skits, called 'Double Vision'. Sir George Head (aka John Cleese) unwittingly proclaims, 'I'm leading this expedition and we're going to climb both peaks of Mount Kilimanjaro,' before Bob (Eric Idle) announces there is only one peak. In fact, there are actually two prominent ones and a third flatter one. Mount Kilimanjaro is mentioned rather memorably in Toto's 1982 hit, 'Africa'. And finally, to dispense with the trivia, in the first trailer for the Xbox 360 game *Halo 3* (ask the kids, trust me!), Kilimanjaro is visible in the background as the lead character, Master Chief, walks along the plains west of the devastated ruins of present-day Mombasa.

These extensive plains surrounding the mountain have an elevation of between 1,100 and 1,400 metres. The only other nearby highlands are a chain of hills running southeast to the coast, the Usambara Mountains, and fifty kilometres to the west-southwest is our isolated volcanic mountain, Mount Meru, above the city of Arusha.

Our trek up the mountain was going to take us on the famous, but less populated, Rongai Route, starting with the departure from the Rongai Gate (already elevated at 1,950 metres) and on to what is known as the First Caves Camp, which is at 2,600 metres above sea level. Having registered at the Marangu Park gate and transferred by Jeep (rather rocky if there's no proper suspension!) we headed on to the Rongai trailhead. This is where we met Reggie, our guide, and his wonderful porters before we began our hike.

The small winding path crosses maize fields before entering pine forest, and then climbs gently. The trail is not at all steep, but is rather a gentle hike through really beautiful country. The forest begins to thin out before you reach the first cave later in the afternoon.

There is much talk of the five ecosystems that you go through climbing Kilimanjaro and you really have to experience it to believe it.

As I meandered, I thought about the Italian Bruno Brunod who, in 2001, managed to reach Uhuru Peak from Marangu Gate in just five hours, thirty-eight minutes and forty seconds. This remains the fastest verified ascent, but at what cost? The risk of pulmonary edema (fluid on the lung) is so immense travelling at that speed to that altitude, but hats off in any case. Our first night's pleasant camp was at First Cave, at about 2,600 metres. There is a toilet and a wooden table with benches, but no hut. Water can be found just down the trail from the camp.

Our second day was memorable as we ascended slowly, 'Poli poli', as they like to say in Tanzania to the Kikelewa Cave that stands impressively at 3,600 metres. We got caught in a spectacular thunderstorm and were hit by giant pieces of hail the size of golf balls falling from the sky. We also met a wonderful group of Americans who were there to enjoy every last minute. I became good pals with two in particular, Amanda from Dallas, who was the secretary of the Dallas Film Board, and Nichole, who hailed from Nebraska and worked as an occupational therapist. They were a great bunch with a great attitude. Just do your best and whatever happens after that is a bonus. Our trail continued up towards Kibo with magnificent views of the eastern ice fields on the crater rim. Day Three saw us depart for the spectacular and rather eerie Mawenzi Tarn camp perched at 4,330 metres. A short but steep climb up some grassy slopes offered us superb views of this wilderness and a chance for the group to practise climbing high and sleeping low. This is the point at which you leave the impressive moorland region behind and quickly enter into what resembles a lunar-like alpine desert that stretches out between the imposing peaks of Mawenzi and Kibo.

Before we even knew, it was the final day before the attempted ascent, Day Four: from Mawenzi Tarn camp (4,330 metres) to the legendary Kibo hut (4,700 metres). We continued ascending on the east side of Kibo, crossing the saddle between Mawenzi and Kibo, and took five hours to reach the Kibo Hut itself. We were in no particular hurry and John, who was relaxed most when he was filming, shot away in this spectacular country, content in the knowledge that I was miked up and that there were plenty of interesting conversations to pick up from those around me. We could feel the wind flapping over us for the first real time as we crept slowly across. The desert seemed to stretch forever in every direction, and the only real landmarks were the jagged Mawenzi behind us and the darker, camel-like hump of Kibo, now straight ahead, so close that we could clearly see the glaciers that crown the top.

The trail is essentially flat at this point, but the direct sun and wind make it a battle against the elements. Sun block and lip balm are critical, along with a constant supply of water or, in my case, a mix of Viper and water. At the end of the day, we camped at the base of Kibo, all visibly anxious, knowing that the most challenging stretch was only a matter of hours away. We rose at eleven that night to eat our food, prehydrate and arrange our light travel supplies.

The quest to reach the Uhuru Peak (5,895 metres) was well and truly on as we made a luminous path with our head torches and walked off into the night. The air was visibly cold. Not for the first time on this trip, I could sense tension in the air. The first section of the trail consists of a rocky path to the Hans Meyer Cave (5,150 metres). I think no more than 10 per cent of those I saw that night even made it that far. People were dropping like flies. They had come unprepared for the altitude and now grown men, who had proud iron-man tattoos on their bodies, were collapsing all around me. Dave was visibly disgusted at the lack of preparation and decided to share his views with John's girlfriend, Anne. He criticised her lack of preparation and the fact that she hadn't acclimatised in her days before we had arrived by doing one of the neighbouring peaks.

True, she hadn't, but was this the time or place for such debate? Reggie intervened and walked behind us at this point with Anne in tow. John was really annoyed. It was hard not to blame him. This was a conversation that could have waited.

We quickly passed people out from that point on as Dave marched us ahead, following our path that zigzagged up to the illusive Gillman's Point (5,681 metres), which is located on the crater rim. This is the point that most people stop at, tired and mentally drained. This section is very steep with a lot of stone scree, requiring a great physical and mental effort. One girl was coming down, visibly shaken and in floods of tears. She wasn't allowed to pass the Gillman Point because she didn't have crampons, the ground up ahead was frozen, and there was a lethal mixture of snow and ice waiting for us at the crater approach.

From Gillman's Point, you will normally encounter snow all the way up to Uhuru Peak, but someone had forgotten to inform Dave about the obvious need for crampons. Perhaps, normally, we wouldn't have risked it, but we had to. We had a record to break and we decided to use the lad's excellent navigational and balance skills to really good effect. I'm not going to lie to you, it was hairy stuff crossing that section of rim. To put this into perspective, no one else from this route appeared behind us. Once we cleared the hazardous section of ice, the sunrise appeared as if to warm our very souls. It remains the most wonderful visual thing I have ever witnessed. Our final section to the high point at 5,895 metres was hassle-free. It was surprisingly cold at the actual summit. I was just relieved that we'd got there. There was no real emotion. I was keen to get off the mountain as quickly as possible and had already started to think about seeing my loved ones at home.

Once I reached the section of scree on the descent, I ran back to the camp. Dave joined me and we raced our Tanzanian porters all the way to the bottom of the mountain. I was on fire and running better than I had in years. There was real speed in my legs and my lungs felt fresh and healthy. It was as if I could feel the transformation taking place as the red blood cells went into overdrive.

Affectionately known as the Coca-Cola Route, Marangu, the route we ran out coming down is by far the most popular route to the summit of Kilimanjaro. This could partly be the result of the fact that the Marangu is the least expensive route. Hut accommodation on it forms one of the main differences, compared to the other routes. It offers you the relative luxury of being able to sleep in huts along the entire route. Mineral water, soft drinks, chocolates and beers are also sold at all the camps on this route. All your equipment and supplies are portered and a cook prepares all your meals. We smiled as we raced past each and every one of these camps.

John and Anne took their time behind us. It had, once again, been a rotten trip for John.

Though he had made his first of the three ascents, he had had nothing but arguments and flare-ups with his girlfriend and witnessed Dave lash her out of it on the final ascent. To her credit, Anne made it to Gillman's Point and would have completed the challenge but for the crampons and a nervous guide who was, in reality, unqualified to guide her without them across the sections of dangerous ice. But for the fact that we needed our permits signed at the last camp section, Dave and I would have been out the gates and in the showers that evening. As it was, lying in the tents that night, I had an epiphany of my own. The girl that I truly loved in my heart, the person who had taught me to feel again, was at home and, despite having been quite selfish up to that point, I was so very desperate to make amends. I felt that I was changing inside, though I still didn't understand how.

The afternoon I arrived back in Dublin for my four-day recovery, I met with one of our charities, Sophia Housing, which supports those with no homes and no self-esteem so humanely. The reality of life at sea level hit me hard that day. Money remained outstanding from various auction winners and tables alike, resulting from the Arctic Ball, the fundraiser we had organised back in November. The night was a great one, a very proud one for all of us. I knew that money from this could be recuperated through making calls and dropping emails, etc., and I got on the case as soon as I left that meeting but there was something far more worrying going on.

The other charity we hoped to raise money for was the Irish Osterporosis Society. The second event, the one that should have given us a real decent leg up in helping both charities, was in real crisis. The Contours in the Park event, which had invited people to do a thirty-minute workout in December in the Phoenix Park, was in a potential loss-making situation. Viewed as a novel means of promoting the Contours brand, while at the same time helping two very deserving causes, the event was organised with the support of various Contours gyms around the country. The number of people taking part had not even approached what had been expected or hoped for by all concerned.

I felt thoroughly ashamed. I really liked the people involved and couldn't for the life of me understand what the hell was going on. Contours was a strong brand that benefited from considerable publicity, but I was the person responsible for the ultimate failure of the event. Leaving the meeting with Contours, the blood and tanned colour drained from my face. I had let down Sister Jean Quinn in Sophia and Professor Moira O'Brien and her people in the Irish Osteoporosis Society. I knew one thing leaving that meeting: no matter what, I simply had to finish this challenge so that I could raise the remaining and promised money on the back of being successful and breaking the world record. People always support you when you make it, right?

꒰꒰꒰

I'm often asked where I get my inspiration from, particularly when things aren't going right for me.

In response, I always try to think about people who have defied the odds in their own special way and come out of their situations more positive for that experience. As it happens, one of my really good mates, Des Mackin, a former inter-county footballer whom I wanted to spend some time with now that I was home for a few days, is an excellent case in point.

Des is five years younger than me but, a fellow Aquarian, our birthdays are a matter of days apart in February. He began playing inter-county for his beloved Armagh back in March 1990 (he'd just turned fifteen at the time). He began minor life as a brilliant and explosive full-forward. You see, as a kid, the person Des wanted to most emulate was Joe Kernan, a former inter-county player himself. Des' father may have been his real hero, but Joe was the man Des wanted to be on the football pitch, the full-forward that he copied to painstaking perfection, the man whose goal-scoring genius he wanted to match.

Joe, in fact, scored two goals in the All-Ireland in 1977.

Just like Joe, Des scored two himself in one of the All-Ireland minor semi-finals in 1992. He was known as a passionate goal getter. He and Diarmuid Marsden were being branded as the 'terrible twins' in their minor days. It was a great feeling and Des' future career looked very promising. Furthermore, when Jim McCory left as manager of Armagh, the talk was all about the two Brians (McAlinden and Canavan), or maybe even Joe Kernan, taking over. It was the two Brians who got the job and brought the team their first Ulster title in 1999 after what had proved to be seventeen long and lean seasons.

On the senior team, Des actually played centre-back over a ten-year period, a decision that surprised many. He missed the 1998 and 2000 seasons due to injury and was left out of the All-Ireland-winning team of 2002, having not been asked to attend any trials or games.

Despite this, as Armagh ascended to their glorious hour in 2002, Des supported them 100 per cent and set all personal feelings aside. Was he gutted? Naturally! But he loved his county. Such was his dedication, that he actually travelled back from his holiday in Miami with his partner Aisling's full support to watch the final because his mates were playing in it, and he knew just how much it meant to them and Armagh people in general.

He watched the game and Armagh won. Their grail was finally eclipsed and Des had tears in his eyes. Some of those tears were for the lads, others for knowing what it meant to them, others were reserved for the simple fact that he had missed out on a historic event in Armagh history.

All people who participate in any sport at any level understand fully the mantra, 'cometh the hour cometh the man'. Des was twenty-seven and in his prime. The hurt was natural. His first reaction was to get down to the pitch and run onto it with open arms; his second thought, to leave the stadium. Finally, Des composed himself, concentrated on his breathing and repeated, 'Why should I miss out on my mates celebrating what I was part of for the past eight seasons?' And so he made his way instead to the players' lounge. He managed to get in without any problem because some of the county representatives knew him and ushered him in. Des looked everyone straight in the eye, but people were sort of shocked that he was actually there celebrating with them. They had just assumed that he would keep his head down because of the way he felt management had treated him.

This was Armagh's day, Des believed, and not his, nor the players', nor indeed anyone's in particular, but Armagh's and Armagh's alone. Inside, he was feeling envious. He stared longingly. His mates had a Celtic Cross and he didn't!

When Des finally met Kieran McGeeney, the captain in charge that day, they hugged openly and said nothing. The tears were in their eyes, for they had journeyed together from Dublin to Armagh (which included Belfast by train) three times a week for three years. They had rented the same house together over this time, so they knew what was required and what it took to bring Sam to Armagh. Each man knew how much it meant to the other. Sometimes, when there is absolute respect, no words are necessary.

Des was invited to go over for the celebration in the impressive City West that night to celebrate with the team, to join one of the tables with Cathal O'Rourke and other members. However, he could not and would not do so and chose instead to arrive when the meal was over. He went around all of his mates and congratulated every one of them. There followed comment from some quarters, 'You should have been on the team', '...or the panel at least...' Words mean very little to guys who live their creed through actions alone. Nonetheless, Des stayed and had the proverbial drinks with one and all. As the night progressed, however, Des could hear the voices in his head, despite trying to concentrate on those around him. He had entered his own personal world. It was not the alcohol. His mind kept telling him, *Des, you can do something about this! But what?* There remained this huge driving force inside of him. He knew the frustration but he also knew that he wasn't going to be there in the same situation the following year. He wanted to affect that outcome. He simply had to. In his heart, the answer became clear. *I can start training tomorrow to get fit and back onto the panel.*

The room was filled with chat of back-to-back titles. When McGeeney, McGrane, Marsden, McNulty and the likes talk about doing something, they are fully intent and focused on only one outcome, allowing their actions to translate those words! You don't speak until you see. You don't visualise until you first believe, you don't believe until you become that very belief itself...

Des walked straight out the door, got in a taxi and went straight to bed. He got up the next morning to train and began to build a training regime that would help to firstly eradicate the prospect of injury. He intended to be flexible and he was planning on being around for the whole season. He incorporated yoga, together with multiple sessions of intense cardio and speed training work to increase his overall fitness levels. He trained every day for three weeks solid and then he requested a meeting.

It was time to meet the boss Joe Kernan. Joe was collecting his Philip's Manager of the Year title one night in Dublin, so Des made contact to meet him the next day in the hotel reception. Upon meeting Joe, Des instinctively congratulated him on bringing Sam across the border to Armagh and asked him what his ambitions were for 2003. He told Des out straight it was to win Sam again.

Joe gave Des three McKenna Cup matches to play before Christmas. One chance to impress the boss, *Do it now, Des, right here, right now.* He played the first one against Down, and scored the winning goal. He played Jordanstown and scored another goal, and then in the third match against Monaghan, which they lost, he – yes, you guessed it – scored another goal, a delicate chip from thirty yards, having spotted the keeper off his line.

The mental resolve that he had got from playing with Armagh from the age of fifteen and with his club Na Fianna in Dublin was standing to him. Stop? Quit? Those words didn't exist in this man's vocabulary. Des knew that if you wanted something badly enough, you find a way to bring it to you!

He had one goal, one clear objective: to be back on that beloved Armagh team. 'If you get knocked down, Ian, get back up. Take it for the experience that it was and take it as the opportunity you were seeking all along. Maybe not that way, but find another.' Des was one of those who utterly believed in me from the very start, from the very first words.

Des Macken may have missed out on the Celtic Cross, but he got the chance to prove that he should have been there, most of all to himself. He played on the team the following season, 2003, in which they lost the final to Tyrone. Perhaps he did not get his golden Celtic Cross, but he got an equally valued silver one. This medal means everything to him, but not in the end as much as finally getting his head together, finding inner peace and going on that journey which required taking plenty of flak along the way, and doing what he had to do.

I knew I was really a very lucky guy who now had a real chance to atone and make it up to the charities. I was going to work twice as hard. And as I prepared for the fourth leg of my journey, I was about to be joined by a woman who would help me make a bit of history for Irish climbing.

14

'It Would Help if You Could Rock Climb!'

'Don't find fault. Find a remedy.'

Henry Ford

Quite apart from the fact that I was, in real terms, a totally novice climber, it's a real wonder that various physical injuries didn't prevent me from breaking down at some stage or another during my world record attempt. As I prepared to head to mountain number four – Carstensz Pyramid – those injuries were eased somewhat by my comrade in arms, Grainne Willis, the first Irish woman to climb the north face of Everest. She preparing to become the first Irish woman on Carstensz Pyramid and was carrying a few hidden injuries of her own.

On Aconcagua, I'd suffered with further severe nerve pain. I'd hardly any teeth left on the upper sides of my mouth but the few that insisted on staying were causing me serious grief. Dr Ciara Scott had kindly arranged for me to see a dental colleague of hers, Dr McEniffe in Terenure, who, very generously and on her own time one Saturday in between my climbs, fixed my problematic teeth.

But, looking back, the real mystery surrounded my knee! I had had a number of problems in final training during those long, bleak winter months of 2006. Earlier that year, following a silly fall which brought my right elbow bone protruding through the skin (just six weeks before we set off on our 100-hour Challenge in June), I had suffered serious nerve-ending pain in my lower right neck (technically referred to as the C5 and C6 areas). The pain was excruciating. I remember dosing up on the strongest regimen of painkillers available on prescription to try and get Professor O'Brien's seal of approval before being sent off to the Island of Skye to do rock and scramble training with Dave Pritt. She knew full well that I was trying to show a range of movement through my arm that I didn't really have at the time, but allowed me to go on the basis that I limited my arm movements. The wonderful therapists in the Sports and Spine Clinic in Dublin had also done magnificent work to even have me in with a shout.

Most of those sessions in Skye ended before lunch with me getting violently sick, but I couldn't afford to miss them, so I went over anyway and did the best that I could. Looking back, it was worth all the pain, as I learned in principle how to do my first rappel on ropes and deal with being on very exposed ground for the first time.

My knees have certainly taken a fair old pounding over the past five years, as you can probably imagine, through one challenge or another. Any sudden or sharp drop in temperature and my right knee seizes up in severe pain for several minutes, rendering me immobile.

During the final gruelling sessions in Glendalough, which included doing press-ups with two Armagh footballers sitting on my back, in the freezing cold and lashing rain, as I prepared to try and peak before the Seven Summits departure, I continued to strain my right calf muscle each and every time I ran out. It was a direct result of a recurring injury to the popliteus muscle, which stretches across the back of the knee. Both Alan Kelly and Enda McNulty, the Armagh full-backs, held out little chance of my being able to board the plane, let alone complete the first mountain.

If Dr Shane Murnaghan taught me how to be proud of who I was, then Enda McNulty, sports psychologist and former All Star footballer, showed me how to win. Enda's methods were orthodox and more rooted in the psychological aspects of winning. Shane had taught me all kinds of incredible things that I was able to bring into play to gain unusual competitive edges. These included using more green peppers in my daily vegetable smoothies to help reduce the build-up of lactic acid as I ran up Camaderry Mountain each and every morning, and stinging my legs with nettles on my longer training runs for similar benefits (this was an Old Native American trick used to great effect by messenger scouts to cover ground efficiently).

Being the modest sort, McNulty would probably say that his contribution to my success was even less than 1 per cent, but that's hardly surprising coming from a man that had to train twice as hard as every other talented player that he grew up with. Not known for being particularly skilful as a footballer, he honed his strengths – natural speed, man marking and tackling – to great perfection. 'It's all about attitude before skill, young man!' he used to say, after putting me through my paces. That maxim was adopted by the boys of Armagh throughout the late 1990s and, despite losing four All-Ireland semi-finals before finally breaking through in 2002, those blood brothers knew how to win.

How many people really know how to win?

Winning, as I've come to learn, isn't about beating the opposition to a pulp or racking up big scores; it's about conquering the battles in your head.

McNulty calls it 'goal setting through not goal setting to'. Why do so many teams or individuals fail to retain their coveted titles, for example? Because they are happy with what they have achieved, right? Their goals have been met. This will become clearer when we discuss what happened to me on Everest but let's stick with sport for just a moment and consider the case of Jonny Wilkinson. The man was familiar with all five match balls before he took to the stage against France in the 2007 Rugby World Cup semi-finals. He requested how many changes of ball during the actual game? He meticulously practised kicking for how long before the actual game? His actions have never wavered, never once despite all the injuries, all the disappointments. Over the past four years, he has been able to goal set through, knowing always that those moments we live for in sport require such focused dedication and that you had better be mentally prepared for them when they do – and believe that they will come. There is no room for complacency and sitting on your laurels if you want to be the very best of the very best.

In business, you might call it clever forward thinking or strategic planning. A company might have five great years as result of the Celtic Tiger. Those companies that remain successful going forward, however, will be the ones who never stopped being proactive even when business was falling into their laps, when they were recruiting extra staff to simply cope with the demand. All the while, there were those who were thinking about the leaner times that would follow.

Enda and Shane used to remind me of the Japanese people whose practices I was somewhat familiar with through sociology and my PR teaching. Japan's post–Second World War economic miracle had its primary roots in the teachings handed down from the codes and ethics of the samurai warriors. The seventeenth-century warrior, Musashi Miyamoto, was the greatest exponent of the samurai way and remained undefeated throughout his life. In his book, *A Book of Five Rings*, which we could all benefit from reading, Miyamoto talked about the philosophy of *kaizen*: the need to surpass tomorrow the person that you were yesterday. It is no coincidence that Jonny Wilkinson is familiar with such practices as *kaizen*, let me assure you.

Perhaps the real reason why my knees had held up to this point on the Seven Summits journey was the fact that, when you are in extreme conditions, other things, like survival, become the priority for the day. Your body can only process one type of pain at a time.

In order to survive, as Enda had pointed out to me, you need to be able to breathe in confidence and breathe out doubt – be in the 'middle of the now', as he put it. One step at a time, one breath at a time.

۞۞۞

Carstensz Pyramid stands at 4,884 metres (16,023 feet) above sea level and it's the only technical rock climb, thank God, within the Seven Summit Challenge. This was the first mountain that John was really looking forward to, where real skill and technique would rise to the surface rather than sheer determination and hard slog. One of the things that would strike me later was how he moved so more efficiently over rock than any of us.

Puncak Jaya, the highest mountain in Australasia and Oceania, was named Carstensz Pyramid after the seventeenth-century Dutch explorer Jan Carstensz, who first sighted glaciers on its slopes in 1623. Carstensz was apparently ridiculed in Europe when he said he had seen snow near the equator, but as Grainne would later testify in her own accounts, even in these days of global warming, there is snow – and plenty of it – in the area.

One of the interesting aspects of the Irian Jaya region (which translates as 'land of freedom', following the departure of the Japanese after the Second World War) as the locals still prefer to call it, rather than Papua, is that it lies just two degrees below the equator and is one of only three tropical mountain ranges with glaciers in the world. It was first climbed by Heinrich Harrer as recently as 1962. Harrer is famous for being part of the first climbing team to scale the north face of the Eiger, but most people know of him from his *Seven Years in Tibet* adventure which provided the basis for the movie with Brad Pitt.

Irian Jaya has over 250 tribal languages and over 800 dialects. It comprises 21 per cent of the total land mass of Indonesia, but is home interestingly to only 1 per cent of its population. It forms one of the last real wilderness areas on earth, something we discovered first hand, with 60 per cent of its territory covered in dense and, for the most part, inaccessible forests.

You only really get this perspective when you are flying high above in the clouds. Its jungle and rainforest is second in size only to the Amazon, and vast tracks of it remain as yet unexplored.

We were due to fly in and travel out with the famous indigenous tribe of the Danni, but, as events unfolded, that hope was dashed. The region has a very diverse landscape in some of the most rugged terrain on earth, ranging from snow-capped mountains to mangrove swamps. Its main resources are oil, gas, copper, wood, naturally enough, and gold. Unfortunately, however, very little of the wealth is shared with the Papuan people. There were times sitting in Base Camp at the bottom of the mountain, watching as the skies lit up eerily below us, drowning in the sound of machines that worked overtime, that I felt there was something really sinister about the world's second-largest goldmine. It lay no more than a three-hour walk from where we were based, and extracted an incredible volume of gold, a tonne a day, each and every day, 365 days of the year.

Carstensz, which is part of the Sudirman Range of mountains, is quite an adventure to reach. The island hopping involved to reach Papua is a marathon in itself – requiring six flights to just get to Nabire on the island of New Guinea, and that was before the helicopter we had booked to take us into Base Camp – but it is official access rather than technical difficulty that is the biggest problem with Carstensz. Political instability and violence in the region have made access extremely difficult in the past and the mountain was closed to outsiders in 2002 after two Americans and an Indonesian were killed in an ambush close to the Freeport goldmine. The Indonesian government only started issuing permits again in 2005.

The morning after we arrived in Nabire (day three), we were up before dawn to head for the small, local airstrip, but the new day revealed lowering cloud and little prospect of an actual take off. The weather gradually cleared and, by half past six, we were airborne, packed into the twelve-seater helicopter with all our gear, plus the fascinating twenty-three-year-old female owner of the helicopter and a couple of workers heading for Enarotali, the first stop on our 140-mile flight.

The co-pilot had briefed us on safety procedures, including wearing our seatbelts and not smoking, so Grainne, John and I were more than a little surprised to see the pilot, inhaling deeply on a cigarette halfway through the flight. Thankfully, he did stub it out before he put on his oxygen mask, as we gained altitude on the way into the 4,000-metre

Base Camp. The image of a pilot smoking and ascending into altitude is one of the classic memories I take with me.

Just before landing, we peered down into the spiralling Freeport goldmine below. As we flew overhead, we saw the heavily laden trucks struggling up the winding roads, sensing their way up out of the murky depths below.

When we finally landed, we were greeted by one of the local tribespeople doing a ritual dance beside the vast green pools serving as lakes. My mind began to drift towards images from *Raiders of the Lost Ark* and stories of head hunters, cannibals and the Stone Age-like tribes such as the Danni, who have only really been exposed to Westerners since the 1960s. Stephen, our local guide for the mountain, arrived shortly after our landing. He'd walked in after several days travelling with the local tribespeople and informed us that there was an unfortunate spot of tribal warfare going on further down the mountain. A dozen or so deaths among the local tribespeople had been confirmed, all within the last week or so. Their gentlemen-like tactics were to be admired, however, as these tribes only fought between the hours of 7 a.m. and 7 p.m.

Costs for the climb ahead were already spiralling. Dave had informed me two weeks earlier that, because one of the clients that he had hoped might be joining us couldn't make it, the price was going to be more to transport us all, $7,000 more, in fact. Meetings with my own bank manager, Vincent McNally, had now become a frequent occurrence, whether by daily phone contact or in person between actual mountains. I was his least lucrative but most demanding customer!

We had first met through my work with Shire Pharmaceuticals. Vincent was from Carrickmacross in Monaghan. Often we would sit and chat for hours about matters of football or rugby. Usually, it was only when the branch was closing that I broached the subject of needing yet more funds to keep the Seven Summits Challenge on the road. I had huge difficulty imagining Vincent trying to persuade the underwriters upstairs that if we didn't get even more money, we could find ourselves in the middle of tribal warfare or, worse still, stuck on this ancient ground with no viable means of escape. That financial support was, of course, in addition to the already extra support that my sponsor Ulster Bank was giving. We had begun, with horror, to see just how out of kilter the original budget estimates were. In the end, and by the time it was all over, the bank would end up finding an additional 50 per cent on top of its original commitment just to keep us afloat. I owed an untold debt of gratitude to people like Sarah Dempsey and Nuala McLaughlin in Ulster Bank.

Carstensz may be the most technically demanding of the Seven Summits, but it is by no means a severe test for anyone with good climbing skills. Looking back, there are a number of things we probably would all agree upon. The food on the trip was appalling, much to both Stephen and Dave's obvious embarrassment. The rations that had been brought up the hill simply didn't cut it. We needed good wholesome food and carbohydrate sustenance but got neither. The second area of mutual agreement concerned the part played by the weather. Had we not climbed the next morning, there's a pretty good chance we simply wouldn't have made it at all. Despite not being acclimatised, Grainne showed little effects of the non-exposure. The following morning when we set off, she was in fine fettle. It took us a couple of hours before first light to reach the base of the actual mountain itself and rope up. I knew she had pretty serious knee problems but decided not to ask too much, preferring instead to concentrate on the endless series of fixed lines we were now about to go up on.

There are three main climbing routes to the summit. The American Direct Route, which goes straight up the sheer Carstensz headwall, looked like a serious undertaking; then there is the long scramble ascent of the East Route and, finally, what is known as the Traditional Route, which is the route taken by Harrer on the first ascent – and now by us, with Grainne and I hoping to become the first Irish people to make it to the top.

The traditional route offers 'good, sustained climbing', as Grainne put it later in her own log 'on excellent but spectacularly sharp rock, with plenty of juggy [sic] hand and footholds'. The exposure is quite extreme on the ridge and there are two fairly serious challenges – the first an eighty-metre vertical wall and the second, further up the jagged, knife-edge summit ridge, is a smooth overhanging wall. The former, I imagine, is a challenging climb for those who enjoy such things, but the latter is thankfully surmounted by setting up a vertical jumar, which is still sheer hell at 4,700 metres.

In fact, I was lucky to make it up that jumar at all, as I found myself leaning into the rock. Grainne tried her level best to support me, while Dave shouted at me to try and step back from the rock face and get a better overall grip. I was so scared and out of my depth, but refused to quit.

It worked by pulling on the jumar with one arm, which was essentially like a locking device, and placing my weight on my opposing foot up into a quickly made looped foothold each time I pulled myself up on the rope. It was bloody hard work and my technique was awful. *Still*, I thought, *I'm not here to win points for technical merit!* I was happy to eventually just scramble over the top and join John who was enjoying himself with the camera. After that, it was relatively straightforward to get to the summit and we made good time, arriving just before 1 p.m. Grainne and I raised the Irish flag proudly, arms aloft. We were chuffed beyond words that we had made it together.

Then the weather, which had felt distinctly clammy to that point, suddenly began to turn. Thick cloud was spiralling across the valley and it was time to depart quick smart. The descent is made easier, of course, by doing a series of abseils which seemed to be going OK until one section of rock, where my rope fell slightly short of the ground below me. What exactly happened afterwards I'm not sure but a screaming match ensued that could have woken the two dead nuns buried somewhere below! Dave and I tore strips off each other, each blaming the other. I simply didn't care anymore, I just wanted off.

As we crossed the ledge before beginning our series of longer abseils off the gully faces, we decided, or John and Dave did at least, to set up a Tyrolean Traverse to get across the deepest chasm, where a 300-metre drop waited for the nervous climber, which, in this case, was me. I was scared out of my wits at the prospect of having to climb across this forty-metre section of rope with two hands and legs strapped on for dear life, moving both arms frantically in an effort to generate some pace. *Do we have to do this?* I wondered. Grainne went after me and enjoyed absolutely every minute of the experience. She wanted to go again, like a little child who had just found Santa Claus perched high on a mountain.

'Mc, you're a bloody sissy!' I laughed. I so admired her attitude, no retreat, no surrender.

John's crossing will stand out in my memory forever. The guy did it SAS-style and was across in a matter of seconds.

Just as we were about to begin the final series of rappels and descents, the heavens opened. I have never seen so much rain fall so quickly or so powerfully. It created a virtual waterfall-like effect, with all the gullies filling simultaneously with water. We got drenched to the skin. But worse was to come. Grainne's knee was hurting her and we had still some way to go when nightfall descended. I'm not sure I would have attempted some of the abseils I did had I actually been able to see where I was going in normal daylight and normal conditions. As it was, necessity was the mother of all invention here and I made it up as I went along.

Dave deserves much credit for somehow guiding me safely off that rock face. Battered and bruised, we began the trip back to Base Camp. Grainne's knee was now gone, shot to pieces. How that woman managed to keep going for the next four hours, I'll never know. She displayed the kind of guts that must have been in real evidence on her trip down the north face of Everest.

The whole experience of doing Carstensz was a little bit surreal. We had gone from doing long treks for each of the three previous mountains to treating Cartensz as a one-day event. Nonetheless, it took two more days to get off Base Camp and negotiate a price for doing so. Grainne kindly stayed on with John for another week to trek over to the other side of Papua, so that we could get that much-needed footage of the Danni tribespeople. I had too much to do back home and needed to raise more funds to keep the show on the road.

The Danni are a fascinating race. A mother, as a sign of grief for a lost loved one, cuts off one of her fingers. Pictures we would get show several of the elder women with maybe only a finger or two left on each hand, with stumps in place of the others. The men live with the animals, namely the pigs, which are considered sacred, and the women live in a commune with the children. It wasn't unheard of for a mother to suckle a baby pig. I was starting to sense that we had something special in terms of the documentary, even if the costs were crucifying me.

One more mountain left before the big one, Ian, I thought. I knew it was going to be tough trying to do a winter ascent of Elbrus, but it would be good practice for the eventualities that might lie further down the line. Right now, it was about coming home, getting things sorted and preparing for a trip to Mother Russia. As I flew into Dublin Airport, preparing to do my radio show on Country Mix, which would be a welcome distraction for the weekend, I joked to the flight attendant, 'Can't be any colder in Russia than the Antarctic, right?' How wrong I would be.

15

From Russia with Love

'What you have to do and the way you have to do it is incredibly simple.
Whether you are willing to do it is another matter.'

Peter F. Drucker

It was 19 March and I had two important tasks to fulfil before I climbed Elbrus – mountain number five.

The first was an absolute pleasure – it's always a pleasure – to present my four-hour radio show on Dublin's Country Mix. The dial mark is 106.8 for the uninitiated among you that find yourselves stumbling across it when looking for Newstalk 106.

I have been doing a Saturday show, called *On the Ball*, on and off for nearly the past three years. It's a mixture of sports updates and easy-listening music. People are often surprised to find that the station plays a wide variety of non-country music. There are the country purists, and there are a great number of them, who listen only to country music but there are also a great number of people who like the easy-listening mix and we have a staggeringly high listenership among taxi drivers, truck drivers and the like. I used to do a Sunday morning show that was far more crossover – lying somewhere between Joni Mitchell and Joan Armatrading – and it seemed to attract lots of new, younger listeners at the time, at least I thought so, judging by the texts that came in.

As far as being a presenter goes, in truth, I'm not particularly good, but I do love it even if that passion has come to me a little late in life. The person who taught me how to actually operate a desk, Lindsey

Dolan, still presents the mid-morning slot on Country. I think it's really important to have lots of really talented women on air.

Among those I have always truly respected in radio is the author and broadcaster Gareth O'Callaghan, formerly, of course, of RTÉ who now does the breakfast show, together with the gifted Ollie Turner, on Galway Bay FM. We had done many compelling interviews together and Gareth's humanity is what makes him such a great presenter, writer and, most importantly to me, friend.

My other passion in life is, and remains, lecturing. I've been at it now on and off for the past ten years and it is still the one thing that I truly love doing in my PR profession. I get more out of it, I'm sure, than my poor, suffering students. Returning to Dublin, I was really looking forward to seeing them all again. We hadn't seen each other in four months, since the climbing began, and they had to tolerate me getting through the course in a very short time before we broke up for the Christmas break. It was now early April and they were no more than six weeks from their exams.

I'm not very orthodox when it comes to delivering those PR sermons from the mount, but one thing we always had, and still do have, is fun in class. I was, however, insistent on three simple rules. Firstly, our classes were wholly interactive. It could never be just me talking endlessly at them.

Secondly, there would always have to be a topic of the day that we might debate other than PR. I'll never forget the wonderful debate that ensued one night between the trade union Impact's very talented information officer, Niall Shanahan, and an equally bright and articulate individual, Nick Becker, who brilliantly debated the merits of blood sports to a packed and attentive gallery. And, finally, everyone's contribution mattered in class, whether you were a legal secretary, bank manager, top PR consultant or simply in between jobs. Everyone had something to contribute where communication was concerned. We all just had to learn to be more open-minded and listen to others.

However, as I stood there in front of the crew that night in Drumcondra doing a quick revision of what we had covered on press release writing, my mind began to drift. We were going through examples of how to make press releases more newsworthy, paying particular attention to the first two paragraphs. The particular example I was discussing related to Adopt Aid. Students had been asked to write a five-paragraph release announcing the set up of this organisation and its prominent role in adoption in Ireland.

We discussed adoption in Ireland and its meaning – i.e. the provision for the permanent transfer of parental rights and duties from the birth parents to the adoptive parents. An adopted child is considered to be the child of the adopters, as if born to them. There had been a significant decline in domestic adoptions in Ireland, from a high of 1,443 in 1975 to 266 in 2002 (167 of these were step-parent adoptions). Today, there are somewhere in the region of 1,200 children waiting to be adopted in Ireland, over 90 per cent of whom are aged between four and sixteen. I was challenging the students on how to overcome, in their releases, the fact that of the 3,000 couples who have registered an interest in adopting, only a small percentage were willing to adopt a child over two years of age. But as my students considered their challenge, my own thoughts were already spiralling and I had started to reflect personally. I could hear those voices in my head, the ones you get when you're nervous and you become conscious of every word that leaves your mouth.

With Everest looming and a winter ascent of Elbrus in Russia upon me, I thought furiously about my own personal circumstances.

Why had I really sought out my birth mother back in 1991? Why, despite having known who my natural father was for over fifteen years, had I never contacted him? Even though he had given me my first break in PR.

It was in his column, after all, that my first-ever press release had appeared (with a photo) back in 1993. At the time, he knew who I was professionally, but had no idea that were linked through blood. Had I any real right not to tell him? What about his wife and children? He had two children, a boy and a girl, and perhaps it was unfair of me to upset their lives. Maybe his wife didn't even know.

As I stood there in front of my class, lost in my own thoughts, oblivious to what was going on around me, I remembered the night I first met Teresa, my birth mother.

It was through the St Patrick's Guild, which used to be based on Dublin's Haddington Road. The Guild helps people like me to trace their natural parents. The process can appear tedious to some. Letters are first exchanged and then contact is made through the appointed adoption officer. The first letter to the mother is cleverly guarded in case of discovery by a third party who, in all likelihood, knows nothing of what happened before. So terms like 'school reunion' are used instead. Of course, the magical date of such a reunion is significant only to the birth mother, in my case 13 February. Incredibly, and much to the surprise of the adoption officer, and to me I might add, Teresa wanted to meet me straight away. It had taken two years to track her down. Contrary to what some people thought at the time, my desire was simply to know where I had come from, to know my roots and my identity. Perhaps there was a touch of *The Bourne Identity*, in that I would wander around sometimes staring at people – on buses, in supermarkets, on trains – wondering if I looked like them, wondering whether they were blood relatives.

I arrived that morning with literally five cigarettes lit, and carrying flowers. *Just keep talking, Ian, that's what you do best anyway.* I was grateful that particular morning, as it happens, for the touch of verbal diarrhoea. Teresa burst into tears when she saw me. She was just so grateful to meet. My heart went out to her, wondering what it must have been like to have carried such a secret all this time, the deception and awful loneliness that she had to face. *But for her courage,* I thought, *I wouldn't be here today.* How difficult must it have been for her? Not being able to track me down the same way that I had been allowed to trace her.

We became instant friends. Good friends too. She's a lovely woman and I consider myself privileged to know her. I think, to be fair, it also helped me to cop on where my own mum was concerned and to appreciate that I had a wonderful mother who had done everything in her power to bring me up well.

One night, Teresa and I had agreed to meet for dinner and I'll never forget what happened.

I had just come from the office of the then Minister for Education Niamh Breathnach, who had kindly obliged as always with the foreword and photograph for our latest edition of the teacher's journal that I had been working on for Avelbury.

As Teresa got into my car, I was telling her the story of being in the minister's office when she handed me a newspaper. 'Your birth father writes for that paper, Ian,' she said. As I turned the pages anxiously wondering who it was, I stumbled upon the page. 'That's him.' My face turned ashen white. I knew him. We'd spoken on the phone!

Thoughts raced back to an earlier final conversation with the minister. As we finished our meeting, she apologised for having to rush as she was facing a press briefing outside. All the press was there. An historic, but contentious, education bill loomed. I could hear the commotion of voices outside the door 'How do you find the press generally, Minister?' I asked genuinely curious.

'They do their job, Ian, and do it well.' Her face smiled that very kind and warm smile of hers. She wasn't one to be easily intimidated or flustered. 'There's one particular journalist, mind you, and we've always had the best of craic. I'm looking forward to catching up with him among the posse outside.' With that, she was gone. I was now staring at that same journalist's face in the paper that Teresa had handed me.

'Hey, Ian? Hello, Walter? Mr Mitty are you there?' One of my students was trying to get my attention and raised a collective laugh from the class.

'Sorry, guys, I got lost in my own thoughts for a while.' As I apologised, a little tear ran down my face. There were so many issues that I hadn't faced up to, but sooner or later I was going to have to.

✿✿✿

Myth holds that it was, in fact, here – on the top of our next mountain – that Zeus chained Prometheus, the Titan who had stolen fire from the gods and given it to ancient man. Mount Elbrus is located in the western Caucasus Mountains, in Kabardino–Balkaria and Karachay–Cherkessia, the heart of Mother Russia, very near the border with Georgia. At the time we arrived, the Foreign Office in Britain was warning tourists to stay away from the region. Tensions were running visibly high in the area.

Elbrus is another example of a stratovolcano that has lain dormant for about 2,000 years. It is the highest mountain in the European Caucasus. Elbrus was on my list of mountains as its west summit stands at 5,642 metres (18,510 feet) and is, therefore, the highest mountain in Europe. The east summit stands slightly lower at 5,621 metres (18,442 feet). Interestingly, the Germans briefly occupied the area surrounding the mountain during the Second World War, with 10,000 soldiers of the Gebirgsjäger, or Mountain Troop, Division. Evidence of the bloody and prolonged battles with their Russian counterparts in appalling, horrendous conditions can still be seen today. Every now and then, for example in times of thaw, the preserved body of a soldier lying face down is found.

The Soviet Union encouraged ascents of Elbrus. In 1956, it was climbed en masse by 400 mountaineers to mark the 400th anniversary of the incorporation of Kabardino–Balkaria, or Autonomous Soviet Socialist Republic, where Elbrus was located. From 1959 to 1976, the cable-car system was built in stages. It brings skiers and climbers alike as high as 3,800 metres to the so-called Barrels. Here you can choose to rest over, in simple but adequate accommodation which provides the climber with an amazing view not only of what lies ahead but also, as you turn around, of spectacular snow- and ice-capped peaks. There are a wide variety of routes up the mountain, but the Normal Route, which is generally free of crevasses, continues more or less straight up the slope from the end of the cable-car system. During the summer, it is not uncommon for 100 people a day to attempt the summit via this route. Winter ascents like ours are rare, and are usually undertaken only by very experienced climbers.

We were being joined on this particular expedition by several new clients of Adventure Peaks, Dave's own trekking company. Two really decent blokes were along with us for the challenge. There was another Dave, a very amiable fireman and former body builder from the Isle of Man, and Will, a charming and talented young climber who was due to turn eighteen during this expedition. Will had high hopes at this stage of becoming the youngest person to complete the Seven Summits, a goal that is as sought after as being the fastest.

We had met up in Moscow with our local guide, the enigmatic Alex, a young, talented climber, tough and focused for what lay ahead. Moscow, I must admit, didn't impress me that much. It's really quite a paradox. There's all the wonderful tourist attractions to see of course – from the Kremlin to the stunning St Basil's Cathedral, whose architect was murdered after its completion so that he couldn't pass on his unique skills to anyone else (best seen at night though when the city is lit up). However, the buildings constructed after the break up of the old Soviet Union do not complement the ones completed during the Brezhnev era. As I stood outside the Kremlin one day, I couldn't help but feel the hotel that appeared as I took a photograph took away from the Kremlin and simply didn't belong there. I felt the same about the towers that mar the landscape behind St Basil's. The people in Moscow, I am sorry to say, are not generally the friendliest either. I got the distinct impression that many of them were walking around with giant chips on their shoulders, quite bitter in their outlook as if the world owed them something. How I wanted to shake them and show them places and townships like Moshi in Tanzania, to see people who had far less but were far happier. Alex remarked that the rest of Russia worked for Moscow, the fastest-growing city in terms of wealth anywhere in the world, where hotel room prices can start at €300–400 a night.

There was a wonderful adage espoused in the times of hardship under Stalin that the people of Moscow pretended to work for the state and the state pretended to pay them. Only when you leave Moscow and travel by car through the bullet-ridden heart of Russia, do you get a real sense of the destitution, seeing the dilapidated buildings and feeling deeply the extreme sense of isolation and poverty. John and I were appalled at what we witnessed and decided we would let the camera tell the real story.

As we soon discovered, Elbrus is notorious for its brutal winter weather, and summit attempts before the end of April are few and far between. The climb is not technically difficult, but it is physically arduous because of the elevations and the frequent biting and viciously piercing winds. The average annual death toll on Elbrus is between fifteen and thirty people. On account of the lads not being acclimatised, we were taking things much more slowly than the previous mountains. Dave had set aside eleven or so days for this particular trip.

On 3 April, the team finally arrived at the Barrels. We then walked up to 4,200 metres and stashed some of our additional kit. The sky was cloudy but the temperatures were more than bearable that particular day, hovering at freezing. The following day, we moved slowly and cautiously up to Purit II (4,200 metres) to sleep before heading back down to the valley on 5 April. Everyone was doing really well, except me. I had picked up a chest infection and was feeling really sick. There was no kick in my movement. It was as if I only had one gear. I decided not to worry too much about it and looked forward to the two days' rest back down in the valley, which was all part of Dave Pritt's acclimatisation plan for the other two lads.

We celebrated Will's birthday in quite a subdued but pleasant fashion, deciding to save the real celebrations until the climb was over, and so we prepared to go back up to face the music. The weather was less kind this time around.

Once back at Purit II, we attempted to get up to the beginning of the rocks of Pastukhov at 4,650 metres, the famous location point for many of the encounters that took place between the German and Russian armies. The temperature had dropped significantly to well below $-15°C$, but with the severe winds scouring our bodies, making the going treacherous, it was more like $-50°C$.

It's difficult to describe the effect this weather has on your body, mind and soul. If you're not feeling very well, you're in very serious trouble and your breathing becomes more laboured by the second, putting added pressure on your heart rate. I collapsed back into the shelter, exhausted; my lungs felt like they were on fire. I was not in very good shape. The left side of my face had been exposed for a couple of minutes whilst talking to camera, and I now had frostbite above my left cheek. I prayed for poor conditions that might buy me another day, though that wasn't going to make any real difference.

That night Will was up and about like a jack rabbit needing two full bottles to relieve himself! I smiled to myself, *Good man, Will, get those fluids into you son.* He had a great attitude and not a trace of ego, which is refreshing in someone his age. Sleeping was tight on two bunks, with three across on each. Icicles formed above our heads, as our breathing pierced the cold air and the wind howled outside, mocking us knowingly, biding its time, aware that we would have to come out sooner or later.

Some twelve hours later, we were up, getting dressed in our full battle amour. Nothing exposed, full balaclavas and face masks, ice axes primed and ready for insertion into the bullet-hard blue ice that we knew awaited up above the rocks of Pastukhov. John was the first casualty. To be honest, I'm sure that everyone felt like joining him when he turned back. The pace was simply too much for him. He had one pace, typical of the experienced guide who saves every ounce of energy in order to last. John operated on the Confucius principle: doesn't matter how long it takes, just don't stop. This time he had no choice because Dave wanted to press ahead. With our crampons fitted, we began the journey into hell, bracing ourselves for what lay ahead.

We were all roped and, as soon as there was too much slack, you knew someone was in trouble. The first three hours of the climb were brutal, steep and endless. The commands from Alex indicated the need to dig the crampons in even harder to avoid any slips in testing, unforgiving forty-five-degree slopes and a curse of a wind to harden your resolve. You just don't want to slip on this blue ice in case you're not able to recover. The level of effort was thoroughly exhausting. One of the bottles I was carrying had split, leaving an orange trail of Viper mix on the ice behind. Looking back, we seemed to zig one way then the next, spiralling upwards into an endless oblivion of blackness and howling winds.

After nearly five hours of climbing through the blackness, we reached 5,000 metres and the route started, finally, to level off. The sun was moody that morning, slow to give us any light. The route became visibly longer by the minute. *Breathe, focus only on the breathing, Ian.* Despite my aching and wretched lungs, mentally I was getting stronger, my resolve was deepening. I was ready to dig and dig again, if necessary. Dave began to look back anxiously every couple of minutes. You could sense his frustration, someone was not keeping the pace he wanted, but who? The rope kept losing its tension. As we reached the saddle just above 5,000 metres, the sun finally peered over the mountains behind us, but it was Dave from the Isle of Man who stopped first. 'Will, are you OK, mate?' He got no response. He went over to the young lad and pulled up his face mask.

Will's eyes were dead. Like a punch-drunk boxer. The kid, to his credit, wanted to continue, but his eyes betrayed his words: it was all over for him. It could have been any one of us. Dave and I looked at each other; we knew the truth. I decided to speak to Dave and tell him we had to go back. 'This isn't worth it. Safety before my ego! We'll get this beast again, I know we will.' Dave carefully examined Will.

Initially, he suggested that we go a little further to see what panned out. I was going nowhere and, eventually, we turned around.

And so it was that on 9 April, we learned first hand a valuable lesson – life can be painfully hard on the mountains. The team had to retreat from Elbrus without the summit. We were at 5,350 metres, with the summit still another two to three hours away. Storm-force winds had stripped the mountain of snow, leaving large expanses of bullet-hard blue ice that would now demand the greatest concentration to climb down.

The correct decision was made and everybody got safely off the mountain. I had absolutely no regrets and the fact of the matter is it simply made me more determined and strengthened my resolve further to overcome all obstacles that were put in my way. So, sometimes life can deal you a hard knock; well deal with it, and move on positively.

Two days later back in Moscow, my wallet was stolen and my phone was cut off again. 'Your back pockets don't belong to you, Ian,' Alex wisely pointed out after five shots of tequila, softening the loss of the €500 and various bits of paperwork. I didn't blame the Russian police for laughing at me at the station. I was feeling sorry for myself when, in fact, it was own stupid fault that I had been robbed.

I knew the challenge had been reasonably hassle-free up to that point. Only the things that truly challenge us in life are worth overcoming. 'God draws straight with crooked lines,' as my pal Caoimhe used to say… Little did I know it, but the challenge to complete this record attempt was, in effect, only beginning.

16

On Top of the World

'You cannot be lonely if you like the person you're alone with.'
Wayne W. Dyer

'Well, George, we knocked the bastard off,' exclaimed the tall, tenacious beekeeper from the southern fringes of the British Empire. Hillary had paused to draw breath and exchange pleasantries with his New Zealand colleague, George Lowe, as he, his Sherpa and Tenzing made their exhausted way down from the world's highest summit. It was 29 May 1953, approaching mid-afternoon, and Tenzing and Hillary had stepped off the highest point of the world at precisely 11.30 a.m., managing to do what no one else had done on the ten previous attempts – finally conquer Everest.

It is them that we had to thank, as we all sat entranced, huddled together watching episode fifteen of series five of the hugely successful American programme, *24*. I sat wondering how our hero Jack Bauer might have fared himself in these conditions, or MacGyver my teenage hero, or Mr Bond, or even Jason Bourne for that matter!

It seems odd to think that at above 5,000 metres the human mind can focus that intently on television and follow such bizarre thought patterns.

We had rigged up John's computer and were watching an 18" monitor in the main mess tent at Base Camp, on the disgusting gravel plains perched just below the Rongbuk Glacier. It was our last couple of days of luxury, back in Base Camp for the final time, as we prepared to return to the hidden world in the clouds above ABC (Advance Base Camp) at 6,500 metres.

John rather cleverly, having been here before, realised and appreciated the need to relieve the mind of the troubles and constant dangers that can surround you on Everest and so had brought several DVDs. *I hope Anne and Lorcan are taping series six back home,* I said to myself. I probably would have texted them to make sure but for the fact that my mobile had been cut off again. There was a booster mast at Base Camp and I decided to ask Keith, one of two Scottish climbers in our group, if I could borrow his phone to call O_2 back home and get it all finally sorted.

I had several other missions that next day, among them making calls to the bank manager and to my parents, completing various media interviews and, most importantly, taking a trip to the extraordinary white bubble tent across the way, which was so huge it could have blocked out the sun. The tent was kitted out with more games, DVDs and music than most people's homes. I had a nervous meeting pending with arguably the most famous man to ever guide on Everest, Russell Brice. To breathe or not breathe (with supplemental oxygen!), that was the question that occupied my racing mind as I lay tossing and turning later that night in my tent.

The use of bottled oxygen to ascend Mount Everest remains as controversial today as it was in the days of George Mallory, the English man who broke the early ground and who even liked to climb butt naked on occasions. Mallory himself described the use of oxygen as 'unsportsmanlike'. Those free-spirited views ended in him only reaching 8,200 metres in his failed 1922 Everest expedition, but he later concluded that it would be impossible to summit without it and, consequently, used it. Following this, he started out on the ill-fated expedition of 1924, which saw both Mallory and his climbing partner, Andrew Irvine, perish somewhere near the summit on 8 June. Mystery still surrounds the one item that has not been recovered, the infamous Kodak Vest Pocket camera, and with it the only clue as to whether or not Mallory made it to the top. Searches for this holiest of grails continue and it remains the stuff of modern-day legend.

When Tenzing and Hillary made the first successful summit in 1953, they used bottled oxygen. And so for the next twenty-five years, bottled oxygen was standard in any successful summit bid. Reinhold Messner, the famous Italian climber who once remarked that you have only half climbed a mountain by reaching its summit, was the first to break the bottled oxygen tradition in 1978, and, with Peter Habeler, made the first successful climb without it.

The world has never been starved of its begrudging critics, let's face it. There were those typically, and perhaps even understandably, who alleged that Messner sucked mini-bottles of oxygen – a claim that incensed the man himself.

Messner was determined to silence all his critics and he finally summited Everest in 1980, without supplemental oxygen or radio support from the Advanced Base Camp, on the even more difficult northwest route. There could be absolutely no doubting the man now. He went on to become the first to climb all fourteen of the coveted peaks that stand above 8,000 metres.

People wondered if his physiology was different to that of other human beings. Was the man super human? Perhaps he had higher oxygen saturation levels than everyone else at extreme altitude? The man – who would eventually return to camp in a fog of exhaustion, totally spent, having fallen earlier in his attempt down a crevasse, but who had miraculously landed on a snow platform – was actually very human indeed. The brilliant studies done by the Cauldwell Extreme Project, which included a team of three Irish doctors, are expected to conclude that it's actually all about the efficiency with which we use the limited oxygen amounts available to us in our blood, rather than the actual levels of oxygen themselves, which are so frighteningly low in the first place.

In any case, in the aftermath of Messner's two successful ascents, the debate on bottled oxygen use raged on.

Jon Krakauer's 1997 book *Into Thin Air* was the first book I agreed to read about Everest. It expressed the author's criticisms of the use of bottled oxygen. Krakauer wrote that the use of bottled oxygen enabled otherwise unqualified climbers to attempt to summit, leading to dangerous situations and more deaths.

The sadly epic tragedy of 10 May 1996, which saw eight climbers lose their lives in a storm, was partially caused by the sheer number of climbers (thirty-three on that day) attempting to ascend. This, in turn, caused massive bottlenecks at the Hillary Step – that forty or so metres of tricky terrain and the last real physical obstacle before the summit on the South East Ridge. Delay here is fatal, as it is on the Second Step, if you chose to climb, as we had, on the North East Ridge.

If the cold doesn't kill you, or at least render you powerless, the concentrated altitude might just do it or the very fact that you are burning precious supplemental oxygen.

And so the bottlenecks that had delayed so many climbers, most of whom summited after the usual 1 p.m. turnaround time, contributed in part to their eventual deaths. Krakauer proposed banning bottled oxygen except in emergency cases. He argued that this would both decrease the growing pollution on Everest (so many bottles have accumulated on its slopes) and keep marginally qualified climbers off the mountain. What Krakauer couldn't prove is that any climber, no matter how brilliant they are, has a God-given right to automatically climb this mountain and not suffer possible death without a constant supply of oxygen. There are simply no studies to show that it's safe to the long-term health of any individual to climb without oxygen. I believe that the decision to use the supplemental oxygen must be considered carefully; ultimately it is for the climber and not guys like Krakauer to decide.

Just because you have climbed above 8,000 metres doesn't mean you will go safely up Everest, or any other peak, with or without oxygen. History has been testament to this on far too many occasions. My own guide, Dave Pritt, who had successfully summited Everest in 2002, would not be successful on this occasion. Instead, as I would witness first hand, he would writhe in excruciating pain, cursed with suspected pulmonary edema at the foot of the North Col.

And so despite all the debates, and in spite of what I have stated above, I was now seriously considering climbing to the summit without supplemental oxygen. I always shuddered as I thought of how Grainne Willis had described coming off the summit onto the Second Step. She tried to abseil with tunnel vision and an oxygen mask that scraped her face. I couldn't tolerate being unable to see peripherally and I decided that I didn't want a mask limiting my vision and fogging up continuously.

But did I seriously think I had any right to such lofty ambitions? Sure, I carried at least a third more haemoglobin in my blood than most human beings. Haemoglobin is the oxygen-carrying molecule in blood and typical values at sea level range from 11.5–16.5 g/l for women and from 13–18 g/l for men. My levels were hitting 18 before I left for the Antarctic.

Haemoglobin concentration increases naturally at altitude as part of the process of acclimatisation and the kidneys regulate for the production of more red blood cells as you ascend higher. I had performed really well on the first trip above the North Col and had managed to climb to just below the rocks at 7,500 metres feeling really good in myself. But, in truth, this didn't give me a free pass and, as I was about to discover, the second time up past ABC can be a wholly different experience.

The following morning at Base Camp, my naïvety was, thankfully, shattered by Russell, who has been leading expeditions to the Himalayas since 1974. He had a regular team of Sherpas who are, together with those employed by Dave Pritt, among the most respected in Nepal. He has led clients to the summit of Everest and Cho Oyu, and also to Himal Chuli (7,540 metres), Shishapangma (8,046 metres) and Ama Dablam (6,856 metres). Russell was there, once again, accommodating the various film crews from the Discovery Channel back to make the second series of *Everest: Beyond the Limit*, which provided a fascinating look at the physical, emotional and psychological challenges involved in reaching the peak of the world's tallest mountain. Overly dramatic in its presentation? Perhaps... but watching guys like Mark Inglis, the double amputee from New Zealand, who became the first amputee to climb Everest, and getting inside the mind of climbers like Mogens Jensen, an asthmatic Iron-Man competitor from Denmark who had plans to climb without supplemental oxygen, made for riveting and compulsive viewing. I had no idea, of course, as I sat talking to Russell that morning that I would end up being part of the 2007 programme.

Brice held the world speed ascent records for the fastest solo without oxygen up Cho Oyu (the mountain that most people like Grainne Willis and Clive, who was in our ascent team, chose to gain experience on before attempting Everest and which is considered the least difficult technically of the 8,000-metre peaks) and Ama Dablam. He was also, in 1988, the first to cross the renowned pinnacles on the northeastern face of Everest. He was one tough man, who, as they might say in Spain, spoke of the bull with great authority, having danced in the ring so many times before. I sat and listened carefully, nodding occasionally. In the end, Russell put it like this. 'You might survive getting to the summit without oxygen, Ian, but I wouldn't rate your chances of ever making its back to Advance Base Camp.' There's a generally accepted rule on Everest that if you haven't been above 8,000 metres before, you use supplemental oxygen, and I'd only been to 7,500 metres.

He may have been tough but Brice, like Hillary before him, did much for the communities of Sherpas and locals whose livelihoods depended largely on the commercial groups that chose to trek and climb through Nepal and Tibet. Over the years, Brice facilitated the building of schools and sanctuaries, and provided much-needed employment to so many.

As I set off the next morning with my backpack fully loaded for the last uncomfortable fourteen-kilometre trip to ABC and another taxing height gain of 1,200-plus metres, I pondered a great many things. I left the Buddhist prayer flags behind me, flapping in the distance, reminding me of the spiritual significance of the final, upward journey I was about to undertake.

Each of us was lost in our own little worlds, with only the rhythmic sound of the bells on the yaks, which carried our supplies, to punctuate our thoughts. Just how Dave and I had put ourselves in with a shout of even getting to the summit in the first place is actually quite remarkable. On Elbrus, we had only reached the same height as Base Camp on Everest. When we first arrived on Everest on 23 April we found ourselves twenty-six days behind the other people climbing at the same time as us in terms of acclimatising. They were already busy acclimatising at the North Col. The day after we'd arrived, we were rocketing up the neighbouring peak, which stood well above 6,000 metres, for acclimatisation practice. The day after that, it was straight up to ABC, with a night pitstop at intermediary camp, which is at 5,800 metres. From ABC, we covered the short distance to the beginning of the fixed lines to the North Col in remarkably quick time, just an hour in fact. We flew up the fixed lines without any problems and got to the foot of the North Col for a night's sleep. Surely it had all been too easy? I knew truthfully that we had only twenty-six days to complete the mission. *Everest is just another mountain, Ian. Respect it fully but you still have two more to climb when you get down!* This was the way I spoke to myself and to the camera for interviews, when I would talk of how much rested on me actually making this mountain for the overall success of the challenge.

Dave had seen a possible weather window forecast for the 14–16 May, so, potentially, we could make an attempt on the 16th. A Swiss team of climbers had planned to do the same. The whole challenge now rested on me delivering in this window. Dave had been courageous to even contemplate giving us a shot.

We had also had bad news concerning Mount McKinley. Dave had spent every night on the phone to Denali National Park trying to secure our permits and entries. We had been refused entry on the grounds that I was making a 'commercial attempt' to set a new world record, even though we had assured them that no money was changing hands. We had told them this was a group of friends climbing together. They were having none of it!

You have to climb McKinley with an American guiding company or you don't get on, and Dave was now desperately trying to find one that might take us on the potential last leg of our journey. As we hadn't enough to worry about right here, right now.

And so, on Everest, together with our ten team members from the main Everest group and a team of very strong Sherpas, we climbed to the North Col (7,000 metres) on 13 May, struggled desperately to Camp 2 (7,800 metres) on the 14th and literally crawled on our hands and knees to Camp 3 (8,200 metres) on the 15th. Everyone chose to be on oxygen above Camp 2 to conserve their dwindling strength for the task ahead. After a few hours of rest and rehydration at the high camp, we planned to begin the final climb at around 11 p.m. This is the most technical part of the route with the infamous Second Step to surmount, but if everything went according to plan we were due to summit at around 8.00 a.m. (which is 3.00 a.m. BST) on the 16th.

There was one woman in our group, Carrie Gibson from Greenock in Scotland. She's five foot nothing, but I have never met a tougher, more determined woman in my entire life. This girl could endure a lot of pain and smile at the same time. Always pleasant and funny to be around, she was quite an inspiration to us all.

Here we were... looking to complete summiting Everest in less than half the normal expedition time, find a permit to complete the world record if we got that far on Mount McKinley, somewhere on the other side of the world, oh and get back to Russia in between all of that – and all of this with half a weather window to work with.

Everyone breathes faster and deeper, hyperventilating at high altitude – it is necessary to do this in order to survive. From twenty to thirty breaths per minute, you suddenly shoot to eighty or ninety. You become aware of the pounding in your head; just trying to breathe is exhausting. As our dwindling group approached high camp, on 15 May and our last foreseeable refuge on this mountain, I was absolutely spent, shattered to my very core. Paul, Dan, Chris, Carrie and one of the guides were still in the race. We had all struggled at different stages above the North Col. There was no word on Clive, one of our group. I assumed that he would arrive in his own good time. Dan, Carrie and I were sharing a tent for the last time before the summit attempt ,which was due to start in six hours.

Tent space is tight up here in the gods. You suddenly become very self-aware as you sit in the tent breathing in supplemental oxygen, trying to relax your body and mind. I thought about the emails I had managed to send before setting off from Advance Base Camp. There was one to an ex-girlfriend that I really needed to send, as if to atone somehow for my ways and apologise for my previous behaviour. I just wanted her to know that I was sorry. Most of the emails were like that, except the one to Sr Jean Quinn, who had kindly sent me a message to wish me well. I wrote back telling her that if I made it, I'd be able to raise the rest of the money for the charity, that people would really get behind me: 'They will Jean, I'll make them, promise...'

Dan and Carrie were up and out of the tent before me, geared up ready for the trip into the blackness of the night and a date with the unknown.

My Sherpa literally kicked me out of the tent, otherwise I'd probably not have come out, such was my exhaustion. The snow was teeming down, reducing visibility to a matter of metres.

Any area above 8,000 metres is classified as a death zone. However, it is significantly more difficult for a climber to survive at the actual death zone on Mount Everest, which is above 8,200 metres. Your body shuts down and you begin to degenerate. In effect, you are slowly dying.

Nothing heals at this height. The longer you are here, the more danger you are in. Temperatures can dip to very, very low levels, resulting in serious frostbite on any body part exposed to the air. Because temperatures are so low, snow is well-frozen in certain areas and death by slipping and falling can, and does, occur, especially when you climb above the First Step. Any fall here and you die.

On Everest, high winds are also a potential threat to climbers. The atmospheric pressure at the top of Everest is about a third of sea-level pressure. About an hour into the climb, we stopped to briefly hydrate and eat a little. My Sherpa handed me some dates, which I took gratefully. Then, suddenly, my body went into convulsions and I was violently sick. The Sherpa was visibly concerned. I was chucking up every valuable ounce of carbohydrate left in my system. He wanted us to turn around. I took off my oxygen mask and looked at him straight in the eye. 'We'll be fine,' I said, wondering where my strength was coming from. 'I'm in good hands. We will do this, my friend. Whatever it takes, we will do this. Trust me.' He smiled back at me and said nothing, turned and began to climb back into the night. I don't even remember crossing the First Step but arrived in surprisingly good fettle for the beginning of the Second Step. I was just focused on my breathing.

We had arrived at the crucial point in the ascent. This is where the record would be won or lost. I was told that the Second Step comprises probably third- or fourth-class rock, more difficult because of the snow on the rock especially in the shade, where it gets very cold. You try not to think about the drops of at least 3,000-plus metres at your feet. It's bloody intimidating.

As I began to make my way up, I approached a piece of rock on a turn that required me to grip tightly with both hands and force my entire body upwards so that I might be able to turn safely. I panicked. I could feel the hot urine running down my right leg. I started to hyperventilate. My Sherpa was already climbing steadily above, out of sight. *What the hell am I doing?* Several dangerous minutes passed while I tried to get my breathing under control. I closed my eyes and prayed. Somebody up there listened to me and my breathing finally returned to normal, whatever normal was. The zone where the Second Step itself is, is over 30 metres high, and continues to twist and turn as you snake your way up it. The Chinese had fixed a bizarre four-and-a-half-metre ladder to the top of the step, with pitons driven halfway in. The ladder is vertical, but twists horribly when you are about halfway up.

Once at the top of the ladder, you have to reach out and negotiate the ropes that lead you up onto the ledge face.

When people ask me about the moment of greatest relief, I say getting off Everest. But reaching the ledge that morning was definitely the second greatest. From there, I actually performed very well.

A long scree terrace leads you to the Third Step, which is an awkward piece of extended rock on the ridge, but very manageable even for a poor climber like me. Above the Third Step is a very steep and long stretch of snow climb, which requires you to kick in methodically with the crampons, as conditions under foot are very hard and icy. The sun had finally come up and everything was now visible in glorious Dulux white.

We finally exited the snow onto the north face, crossing a long, narrow ledge which leads to a rock groove that finally takes you up to the summit ridge. I couldn't believe the levels of concentration required or the nature of the steep and awkward ground at this point. The actual ridge seemed to go for an eternity, over undulating ice and snow. However, there were spectacular cornices to admire on the way to the roof of the world.

I stood there, at first perplexed that I had actually made it. Our guide joined me, followed by Chris and Paul. Dan and Carrie had already been to the summit and we had passed them earlier, smiling proudly. The next thirty minutes of my life were spent in a very pleasant, but surreal environment. The first climbers from the southeast ridge joined us and there were tears and celebrations. Satellite phones were out and calls to loved ones followed. My only thoughts, strangely, were to phone my pal and co-lecturer Eugene, who was handling the PR back home, so he could let the media know that I'd made the summit. I hoped that more people would go on to the website and make contributions to the charities. I was proud, of course I was proud, but only two thoughts filled my mind. Getting back to Base Camp safely and completing the overall mission.

If going up seemed too easy by far, then coming down Everest remains my greatest accomplishment to date. Where to start?

Getting tangled up in the ropes coming off the Second Step which required my rucksack to be cut dangerously with a penknife while hanging off the Chinese ladder? Falling continuously on the mixed terrain while I was still in the death zone? Trying to descend, or simply surviving without any sight for days and making my way back to Advance Base Camp completely blind?

I went snow-blind the moment I entered the tent at 8,200 metres, thinking that I was just going for a short rest before beginning the long descent. The pain was, at first, excruciating. Snow-blindness, a severe burning of the eyeball, happens either as result of cerebral edema or because your eyes have been exposed to the blinding snow for too long. Hanging on the ladder, I lost my sunglasses, and, for at least four to five minutes, my eyes had clearly been exposed. I also regret not wearing my sunglasses the previous night as the snow had poured down.

At one point, on the fixed lines as we set out the next morning, I tripped over the body of a Czech climber.

A Canadian climber approached me when he saw me fall down the lines for twenty metres or so. He had seen me fall over the dead body and noticed that my appointed Sherpa was someway behind me. He noted my oxygen supply and warned me that I was in severe danger and that I was killing my Sherpa, who was carrying a load in excess of forty kilos. I thanked him for his advice and apologised that I couldn't see him. We travelled no more than another twenty minutes before I fell again. This time I fell to the ground and cried out loudly. I knew the situation had become hopeless. I was killing this poor guy behind me, who was trying desperately to save my life. I sat on the ground, shaking furiously and prepared myself to die. I was going to let the Sherpa move on and I would stay. I thought of my friend Mirka, a Czech doctor who lived in Brno in the Czech Republic. I had no idea at the time that the dead climber who lay somewhere above me was her colleague.

I decided that I would put on my Sony Walkman and let it just play itself out; whatever charge was left wasn't going to last long up here. I was now totally accepting of the fate that awaited me. There were no regrets. Fumbling with the Walkman, I could barely make out the long and distinctive guitar introduction to 'Give Me Shelter' as it wound into the powerful accompanying female vocal. Then, just as Mick Jagger's voice came into the song, I felt something stirring inexplicably inside me. A voice inside my head told me to get off the ground and stop feeling sorry for myself. *Get out of the death zone, and ask the Sherpa to get on the radio and ask for more help. Be calm, breathe and be.* Where was this inner strength coming from? The inspiration to change; the will to suddenly want to live again?

It seemed like everything was suddenly happening at warp speed.

Nuru and his team of incredible sherpas saved my life that day. Somehow, they helped to get me and Clive, who had also fallen behind through sheer exhaustion, all the way to the foot of the North Col for a night's rest. Here our other guide was able to take over to get me slowly down the fixed lines and back to Advance Base Camp. I was treated by Russell's doctor, a wonderful lady, who slowly helped to restore my sight over the coming days. A huge debt of gratitude must go to Dave Pritt for handling the whole operation back at ABC.

I can only imagine the nerves he was feeling. I was now fully focused. I was fully intent on completing the Seven Summits Challenge. I promised myself that, one day, I would repay the courage of those incredible men who put their lives on the line every day on Everest, fixing ropes, carrying incredible loads, so that guys like me get a shot at being famous for a day and breaking world records.

Let us never forget, the Sherpas are the real heroes on this mountain – humble and humane to the core. I owe them my life.

17
'They Think It's All Over, It Is Now!'

'The best thing about the future is that it only comes one day at a time.'
Abraham Lincoln

I have two good mates, who both happen to own restaurants: Dominico, who owns the very successful Italian eatery, Picasso's in Clontarf with his wife, Claire, and Tom Corcoran who owns a restaurant in Monkstown called Siam Thai. Both of these fine eating establishments fed me frequently before and during my Seven Summits Challenge, for which I am grateful. The day I arrived home from Everest, with a week to recover till we went back to Russia, I received a phone call from Tom Corcoran.

After congratulating me, he informed me that he had gone in on a deal with two mates of his and bought a hotel, Glencar House, in Glencar, County Kerry, which sat overlooking Carrauntohill Mountain. Tom assured me that the views were magnificent but he was embarrassed because he had never been up the mountain himself. He was, understandably, worried that he wouldn't be able to offer genuine advice to his hotel guests on which routes to take up the mountain. After all, he and his mates had bought this hotel for one primary reason: they were passionate about hillwalking and wanted to establish Glencar as the place that would become synonymous with climbing Ireland's highest mountain. 'So will you bring me up the mountain, Ian?

I laughed with Tom, 'Sure, what else would I be doing during my recovery? Course I'll bring you.'

Standing at the cross on the summit that beautiful Wednesday afternoon, I felt very proud to be there with Tom. I was amazed at how my feet were able to seemingly glide over ground and I felt like I was somehow hovering at times, never once out of breath. At the summit, we phoned Tom's wife, Clodagh – a woman that some in Tom's circle had described as 'a beautiful woman with just a whiff of danger about her'.

Oh it was good to be back in Kerry and among Kerry folk! This was a very special place for me. We stayed for what seemed like hours, chatting to the Cronins at the foot of the mountain, recalling old stories of the mountain and how, one day, I had this dream to break the record for the Five Peaks. That all seemed in the very distant past.

On the picturesque journey back into Glencar House, I managed to leave the oil sump of my car nestled on the cattle grid that greets you as you turn into the hotel. I was leaking more oil up the long driveway than a sheik's barrel. Nevertheless, we had a wonderful night of craic and devilment, amusing ourselves by the bar in front of the open fire. Tom lent me his car to drive home. We'd figure out how to get my car back to Dublin some other time.

Although I had always kept my gym visits up in between mountains, something felt different this time round. I was acutely aware of the red blood cells working overtime in my body. I felt remarkably good, despite losing yet more weight. I had lost eighteen pounds and was now down to eleven stone, seven pounds. *The lightest I've been since school,* I thought to myself.

Despite losing all the upper body muscle, my legs were incredibly strong and my resting heart rate had dropped to below forty beats for the first time in my life. I wondered just how fit I had become. I decided to pay the old UCD racing track a visit, for old time's sake, and run a 100 metres for the sheer hell of it. I clocked 11.3 seconds. Often when you pass the sixty-metre point on a 100-metre sprint, you can feel yourself unable to maintain the core speed. On this particular occasion, I didn't notice any changes except an inexplicable desire to keep running! In the gym the following day, my five kilometres on the treadmill dropped below eighteen minutes. I was on fire and it felt fantastic. I knew, of course, that it would only last for a certain amount of time. I felt like one of the old guys in the movie *Cocoon*, when he gets a sudden resurgence of life and is able to do the things he did as a youngster, only better.

I tried to see as many people as I could when I was home that week. I spent time with my mates, Des and Aisling. I spoke to Des about the letters that I had taken up each mountain, including his own inspirational letter which had helped me up the first mountain all that time ago and the marvellous letter my old pal Caroline McIntyre wrote for me with her son that inspired me on Everest.

I spoke with Shane, Grainne, Ciara and Enda, too. I also made sure to check in with myself, knowing that I still had two mountains to climb back to back and not wanting to get any notions above my station. There was still so much work to do and it would only take one moment of arrogance to bring the whole house of cards tumbling down.

On 28 May, as I stood outside Moscow International Airport, I gave my finest interview on radio to Pat Kenny. We spoke of the snow-blindness and how Dr Bobart, attached to the Adelaide Eye and Ear Hospital, had generously helped me back to recovery, for no charge or fee. A mutual pal of ours, Declan Kennedy, who was on board to support our documentary, had kindly hooked us up. Apart from a few dry spots and some corneal damage, I assured Pat and the listeners, my eyes would be fine, as long as they were never exposed again to sunlight on a big mountain. Pat asked me how long I thought it would take to summit Elbrus. I told him a day. 'A day!' he replied incredulously.

'We've no time to waste, Pat. I hope to have news for you tomorrow.'

So it was that, in the early hours of 31 May, we summited Elbrus in proud fashion. We tore up that mountain as if our lives depended on it. This time, myself and Dave who, to his credit, was recovering well despite the edema, left Alex in our tracks as he struggled to keep pace with us. The weather was a lot kinder this time; the snow was more manageable and the bullet-hard ice was gone. However, to do what we did in that trip – land in Russia, travel to the Caucasus, trek and summit, all within a period of fifty-odd hours – was truly inspiring. It was made all the more incredible to think that we were only a week or so home from doing battle with the mother of all mountains, Everest itself.

There wasn't a moment to lose. John was busy back in the UK going through footage and preparing to join us on the final leg, and there was much that needed my final attention back home, which mostly revolved around securing additional finance. The bills – for the constantly changing flights, the one-on-one Sherpa assistance, the bottled oxygen, getting John off Everest and Dave's extra time shooting film on Elbrus – continued to add up, not to mention the fact that just going back to Elbrus itself was costing me another €6,500.

I was long past caring about the cost. There was a far bigger picture to think about, a potential new world record by an Irishman and the world's first-ever documentary of the Seven Summits. No debts, borrowings or cranky underwriters were going go hold us back. Vincent McNally, John Nolan and the sponsorship team at Ulster Bank continued, therefore, to wave their magic wands to keep the show on the road.

❧❧❧

On the morning of 14 June, we arrived in a suburban back garden, deep in the heart of Anchorage, where the team meeting for Mount McKinley was taking place. Until then, we hadn't actually known whether John had a permit to accompany us up the mountain. Dave, our American guide from Mountain Madness, informed us casually after that meeting that, of course, we had and wondered why we didn't know ourselves! *Thank God,* I thought. Quite apart from the reported beauty of the mountain that lay ahead and capturing it on film, John was a mate and I wanted him there to share in whatever experience might lie ahead.

Alaska is a stunningly beautiful country. The registration plates on the cars carry the words 'The last frontier' and remind the visitor of just how remote this vast wilderness really is.

Mount McKinley is located in the central portion of the Alaska Range, which spans much of south central Alaska. It is approximately 208 kilometres north-northwest of Anchorage and 248 kilometres southwest of Fairbanks. Given that the summit is approximately thirty-five miles plus from the nearest major road, the George Parks Highway, we decided to drive to the nearest town, Talkeetna, and fly across on the twin-engine Otter from there. Once again, we were back with a large group of people and, once again, there was only one female climber among us, Lei, a Chinese climber, who hoped to become the first Chinese woman to complete the Seven Summits.

It was a really cool group of people, in fact, which comprised a core team of six Americans, including a father-and-son team, two Germans (Christian, a highly intelligent senior official with the German government who modestly never used his doctorate title), and Stefan, a happily married architect from Cologne whose wife, we later learned, owned more shoes than Imelda Marcos and commissioned a special wardrobe emporium from Stefan to show those shoes in their fullest glory.

The two guides assisting American Dave to oversee the trip were fascinating characters. Pablo, who came from Ecuador, was the ultimate cool dude, *'¿Hey dude, cómo estás, amigo?'* was how he cheerfully greeted everyone, every morning, irrespective of the weather or the problems we were facing at the time. The second guide was Zach, a gifted twenty-seven year old who lived in Alaska. His technical knowledge about climbing, rafting – in fact, most sports – was quite overwhelming. He was certainly an old soul in a young body. Incredibly strong physically, he had returned forty-eight hours before we set off from an attempt up McKinley to co-guide with us, despite the last mission ending 1,200 metres below the summit due to weather conditions.

They talk a great deal about the weather on this mountain. Conditions here can be the worst you are likely to experience anywhere in the world, including K2. The boards in the Ranger's Office when we arrived in Talkeetna didn't bode well. Of the thousand or so attempts, so far this year fewer than one in three had summited.

It took us nearly four days for the weather on the mountain to improve sufficiently to allow the small planes in. Not that I minded, as I'd found the most amazing strawberry cheesecake anywhere on this planet up the road in the famous West Rib pub. I didn't have enough money for accommodation, so I slept in the hanger, as did John. It was peaceful under those stars. Next door to us were some old bunks, but they had been taken by a team of Japanese climbers who were flying out at the same time as us.

Mount McKinley is also commonly known as Denali, which translates as 'the high one' in the local Athabaskan language. It is the name currently recognised by the state of Alaska. In 1896, the mountain was officially named Mount McKinley, after the former Governor of Ohio and future US President William McKinley. Personally, I prefer the name Denali, as it means so much more when you stand on a clear day looking across at this truly majestic peak. It was, without doubt, the most beautiful mountain I had ever seen.

Also flying out at the same time as us was a group of English doctors with whom I would become good pals. Each of them had resigned their respective commissions in the Royal Air Force, Marines and Paratroopers to go back to college to become doctors. They were all in the early to mid-thirties, and a more contented bunch of lads you couldn't hope to meet.

As we eventually flew onto the great mountain, I was reminded of the fact that Denali has a larger bulk and rise than Mount Everest. Even though the summit of Everest is about 2,700 metres (9,000 feet) higher as measured from sea level, its base sits on the Tibetan Plateau at about 5,200 metres, giving it a real vertical rise of little more than 3,700 metres (12,000 feet). The base of Mount McKinley is roughly a 600-metre plateau, giving it an actual rise of 5,500 metres. You truly appreciate this rise as you gaze in wonderment at the five spectacular five glaciers below, as they twist and turn impressively up this beast of a mountain. We were interested in the Kahiltna Glacier and were taking the eighteen-kilometre Western Buttress Course, the easier and most standard route to the top.

The first ascent of the main summit of McKinley came on 7 June 1913 by a party led by Hudson Stuck. The first man from that party to reach the actual summit was Walter Harper, an Alaskan native. One of his climbing colleagues, Tatum, later commented, 'The view from the top of Mount McKinley is like looking out the windows of heaven!' They had ascended by the Muldrow Glacier Route pioneered by the earlier expeditions, which is still often climbed today. By 2003, the mountain had claimed the lives of nearly 100 mountaineers.

The vast majority of climbers, like us, use the Western Buttress Route, which was pioneered in 1951 by Bradford Washburn, after an extensive aerial photographic analysis of the mountain. Climbing this mountain, they say, typically takes two to four weeks. Looking back, and I say this with no intended arrogance, it could really be done in less than a week – if the weather is with you, if you're fit and acclimatised and if, like me, you're crazy enough to treat all mountains on the same principle, that it's one foot in front of the other. That's a lot of variables and, in truth, when you bring together a random group of people on a guided trek, the one variable that you really cannot count on, apart from the weather, is the fact that everyone could not possibly be equally acclimatised. Trust me when I say that the difference in performance between those who are acclimatised and those who are not is a little bit like asking a schoolboy rugby team to do battle with the All Blacks.

There are three valuable lessons to take on board when climbing this mountain. Firstly, the climb has a tremendous physical impact on your body. You pull full sledges and carry full rucksacks on your back considerable distances each and every day, usually till you get to 4,300 metres, over terrain such as the section of ice and snow aptly named Heartbreak Hill. The heat on these glaciers can be overwhelming. We were subjected to ferocious temperatures as the sun beat off the blue ice, forcing us to strip off layers of clothing – on occasions to few or none.

Patience is the order of the day if you are climbing in a group convoy. John was understandably happier with the slower more methodical pace that American Dave had set. I'd be lying if I said, after nearly five months of physical and mental torture, that I wouldn't have liked it to quicken up, even slightly. But therein lies the second lesson for most people: this mountain is characterised by an unusually severe risk of serious altitude sickness for climbers (as poor Stefan was about to discover) due to its high elevation and its high latitude. At the equator, a mountain as high as Mount McKinley would have 47 per cent as much oxygen available on its summit as there is at sea level, but, because of its latitude, the pressure on the summit of McKinley is considerably lower. Dave was a wily old fox, who'd been there and got too many T-shirts and didn't tolerate heroes. I was careful not to push my exuberance for a possible new speed record. In truth, we were really lucky to be on the mountain at all. Had I not summited Everest on 16 May, this attempt wouldn't have happened because this was the only available date we would have been allowed on. Even news of that permission hadn't become clear until I had stumbled blind into the Advance Base Camp nearly three weeks earlier.

Everything went swimmingly until we got to High Camp at 5,200 metres and the weather turned four shades of nasty. There were mornings when I woke up and scurried across to the makeshift toilets (elaborate holes in the ground), I could feel an extreme stinging pain in my fingers. It remained lethally cold for the best part of a week.

You certainly get to know the people you are climbing with pretty well in such close quarters. We had curious and intimate conversations about anything and everything. One day, Tom, a really funny guy and local bear hunter who was sharing with myself and John, asked me to name the following: the best present that I had ever given anyone, the proudest professional moment of my life and the people that I most admired and why. The best present brought a warm smile to my face and reminded me of a world that I seemed to be no longer a part of.

My mind drifted in time to people and places back home.

What do you give someone who has everything? Gerald Kean, the larger-than-life solicitor who is written about frequently on the social pages of Irish papers, is actually one of the nicest and funniest blokes I know. I really couldn't care about his personal wealth, or the things people say about him – often people who don't even know the man. Instead I prefer to reflect on the very generous man, with a real heart. When his daughter Kirsten was celebrating her fourth birthday, I didn't know what to buy her, and I didn't exactly have the riches of the world to call upon. An old photographer friend of mine, Tom Lawlor, one of the very best press clickers in the business who used to be with *The Irish Times*, kindly obliged me with a splendid favour.

We sort of kidnapped Kirsten one afternoon and brought her, in tow with her nanny, to Bushy Park in Terenure. Tom watched and waited as she played on the swings and danced happily in the warm sunshine. I was worried that he wasn't clicking his camera. Tom was a patient man and knew what he required. About an hour later, as Kirsten was making her way around the park, she spotted two old men playing the French game of boules. As she approached them to hand back a ball that had strayed onto the path, I heard the camera click, once, twice and then a third time. Tom smiled happily and announced that we were done. Gerald Kean, for all his immense wealth and success, treasures the birth of his daughter as his proudest moment and the pictures from Tom remain dear to him to this day.

Muhammad Ali and Andre Agassi are the two sporting heroes in my life. The latter, who is the same age as me, remains the only player in the open era to have won every Grand Slam singles title, to have won the Tennis Masters Cup, to have been part of a winning Davis Cup team and to have won an Olympic gold medal. He also came back from the dead to remain hungry enough, to want to put his body through the pain and torture to climb up the rankings and get his eighth and final Grand Slam back in 2003. I carried a picture of Agassi in my wallet to remind me every single day that anything you believe is possible, truly is.

Tom appreciated the vote for a fellow American and asked once again about the professional moments. Well, the person I most admire professionally is Professor Pat McKeon, the current head of St Patrick's Hospital and the founder of Aware Defeat Depression. Pat once famously remarked that until we, as a society in Ireland, radically review both our attitude towards and treatment of depression, we could not hope to reasonably bring down the alarming suicide rates in this country. As my proudest professional moment, I could pick anything that we did together over a three- or four-year period, including the excellent work with Seamus Dooley and the NUJ to provide important media guidelines in the reporting of suicide. But the memory that I remain most proud of, and humbled by, is the inspiring series of talks that we ran the length and breadth of the country, North and South, with a group of six incredibly courageous young individuals, all of whom had attempted at one point or another to take their own lives.

❧❧❧

Good things come to those who wait, isn't that what we are supposed to believe? Eventually, despite several false starts, including the trip to the saddle that resulted in Stefan being brought down with suspected cerebral edema, we finally got the green light on 29 June to begin our final ascent to the summit of Denali.

We had agreed to split into two groups at the saddle. Here the winds turn nasty and the climbing becomes steeper and slightly more technical for about an hour or so as you ascend through mixed terrain.

Dave, myself and Christian were allowed to forge ahead, fearing that it may be our last opportunity to make it. They were clearing the Base Camp in anticipation of getting the last climber off the mountain. The crevasses were beginning to open, making the trek back to Base Camp very hazardous in many spots.

Summit day, 29 June, on Denali is well and truly earned. Although the famous 'football pitch' of snow and ice comes into view within an hour and a half of ascending above the saddle, the actual time required to reach it is misleading. There is an endless series of hills and snow plains to cover first. Then, when you finally arrive below the long and tricky summit ledge, you have another hour or so of steep ice to negotiate and have to zigzag in endless weaving patterns before you finally step onto the exposed ledge. By the time we made the ledge at about 11 p.m., the weather had turned poorer, with visibility reducing by the second. Christian and I were more than a little nervous and extremely tired mentally. There are deadly sharp falls and drops either side of the ridge. We slowly continued on our way, negotiating across the fifty-minute or so journey to the summit point, roped up, ice axes clenched firmly in hand.

When I finally reached the slightly raised point of ground, hidden as we weaved and turned anxiously over the final stretch of rock and ice, I fell on my knees with my ski pole above my head. I wept openly, shaking in sheer relief. Though the long and exhausting journey home awaited us all, it didn't matter any more. Who the hell cared? It was finally over.

ধধধ

At 4 a.m. local time, the phone rang in my hotel bedroom. I was sleepless in Seattle, for sure. I had done a few pieces for radio stations back home, so didn't mind talking to anyone about anything. Besides, it was the morning before I was due to fly home at last to my family and friends. I was off the mountain and resting up for a few days in clean bed sheets, and was clean myself for the first time in months.

It was my buddy Eugene on the other end of the line, the man who had stood by me through thick and thin over the course of nearly twenty years, the man who had stood as my best man back in 1997. The man for whom I now lectured in PR and, most of all, the man who is my friend. He was the guy who appreciated, more than any other, the sheer magnitude of what we had just accomplished. 'Be proud in this moment, Ian. What you have achieved is something your grandchildren will pass on to their grandchildren.'

The world record of 187 days had been smashed, torn to shreds by an incredible thirty-two days and the world of mountaineering, for a day at least, had been turned on its head by a Paddy. Things that we only dreamed were possible for a chosen, select few had suddenly become achievable by an ordinary guy. This was my moment. I had come of age in every sense, finally I had come to realise that you don't have to climb a mountain to conquer your own Everest.

Post Script
There's Always a Choice

'A man travels the world over in search of what he needs and returns home to find it.'

George Moore

I travelled on autopilot to Australia with John and completed my eighth and final summit on Snowy Mountain, eclipsing by two days the second record set by the Indian climber Mabu for the alternate version of the Seven Summits. So, on 11 July 2007, I became the first person in the world to hold both world speed records simultaneously.

I had finally ended my epic journey on the mountains, standing in wind chill temperatures of −20°C dressed in a full tuxedo. The Black Tie Group had offered to sponsor me if I wore one of their dress suits at the top of the bottom of the world, capturing the notion that it was important to look and feel one's best at all times.

One hundred and sixty-nine days of gruelling highs and lows were now finally at an end.

I knew that a sponsor would be required to get us over the finishing line. The day I arrived home the news came through from one of the companies that we had pinned our hopes on, the ESB, that they couldn't support our documentary and provide us with the finishing funds we needed to complete the project. To be fair to the ESB, they loved the match of man and his epic struggle with nature but the timing was just wrong. And as the bills came tumbling through the door, the full extent of the debts I now personally owed became frighteningly apparent. Between debtors, credit cards, loans and phones, it was looking like something in the region of €75,000.

I suppose, looking back, it would have been easy to just lie down and feel sorry for myself, and for several weeks after coming home I did just that. But, thankfully, a series of amazing things happened that gave me back my compass and restored my faith in the things that matter – family, friends and health.

I have no children but if, one day, I should be blessed to have some, I hope that they are as inspiring to me as my wonderful godson and nephew.

My godson Sean, or 'Seany' as I call him, grew up in the States and was keen to climb a mountain. Kids are wonderful because they crave only love and affection from those people that they care about most. They forgive you for the times that you are not around or have let them down in the past. I had missed out on Sean's growing up to that point and had lost touch with him. I was determined that would never happen again. His mum, Noleen, and I have become very close pals and I was grateful to be given a second chance to get to know her two wonderful children – Sarah, who was bright and beautiful and already fourteen, and Sean who was nine.

The day I climbed Carrauntohill with Sean in September 2007, I will remember for the rest of my life. Above the Devil's Ladder, the visibility had turned poor. An Australian climber was descending and told me that visibility was about ten metres or so to the summit. I wasn't sure what to do. The next thing Sean piped up, 'Hey, Ian, did we come here to climb the mountain, or what?' He strode ahead of me, leading the way. As this nine-year-old boy stood at the top, I felt immensely proud to be his godfather. His guts and determination put me to shame. As I came down the summit, slightly ahead of him, I had a tear in my eye.

It had taken this kid to awaken in me a sense of personal pride and the realisation that spending time with the people you love is priceless.

Coincidentally, my sister Denise's son, Andrew, was enjoying his first year at Presentation College in Bray, where Sean's Uncle Johnny taught Maths and Science. Andrew would turn thirteen at Christmas and was an extraordinary young man, who knew more about sports, cars and movies – in fact, just about everything – than me, Denise and her partner, Paul, combined. He was due to play in the final of the McCorry Cup. The cup was a kind of showcase of potential rugby talent and was played out by the various classes in first year. Andrew's class had made the final. The last time I had seen him, he was playing footy and now, thanks to the wise influence of Paul, he was playing rugby. Paul told me there something special about Andrew's awareness on the rugby pitch.

He made Peter Stringer look like a giant. But what he lacked in physical stature, he more than made up for in heart, quick hands, a superb pass and a wonderful brain that was made for playing out-half. Mark my words when I say that Andrew McKeever has the ability to go all the way. Watching him play in the final that day, I couldn't contain my excitement. He got hurt a few times but always got up and never quit.

How lucky am I to be a small part of these kids' lives? I never fully appreciated till those two days the wonderful joy that children can bring to your life.

It got me thinking about all of my friends, the ones that I hadn't spent enough time with because I was always too wrapped up in my own selfish little world. I thought about Dave Burke and his wife Sandra, who is expecting their fourth child. And I thought about the sacrifices they make for their children.

I really had nothing to complain about. Sure I had debts, but they would eventually sort themselves out and now I had real opportunities to help other people conquer their own Everests. I just needed to step back from the trees around me and take stock.

I sat down and thought carefully about the goals I wanted to achieve. First, I wanted to present another radio show. I had this idea coming off Everest of taking *Reeling in the Years* and giving it a treatment for radio. I approached Anna Leddy head of RTÉ Radio and she kindly commissioned a pilot, giving me Pat Kenny's radio producer Conor Kavanagh to work with.

I told Eugene Grey that I wanted to go back lecturing. I also wanted to do some motivational speaking. I knew that, in my heart, I had seen both sides of the equation. I knew what it was like to need help and I knew what it was now like to be able to help others. I knew that my experiences and learning could really help other people. And besides, if nothing else, I was bloody good talker!

I got my first break with PricewaterhouseCoopers thanks to Margaret O'Gorman, the head of marketing, who had read an article about me in *The Irish Examiner*. Standing in front of the cream of Irish accounting and auditor talent inspired me even more. The feeling in the air that afternoon was the kind of thing you would want to bottle and pass on.

Good pals of mine in Cork had kindly organised a golf classic through the Mitchelstown Golf Club to support my chosen charities: Sophia Housing and the Irish Osteoporosis Society. I decided that I would also give a large percentage of the fees I received for giving talks. This would help me to reach that figure I had originally set myself. I knew now that the Seven Summits record challenge was really only beginning. I was reminded that we can only ever take one step at a time... I knew that Confucius was right. It was going be a slower process than perhaps I would have liked but I wasn't ever going to stop.

As I write this, I am recovering from the wonderful Wicklow People in Need Ball. There, I got to spend time with the people who inspired me when I set out fifteen years ago in my PR career, people like Ellen Gunning, who made me want to lecture, Janice Ashmore Ryan, Eugene Grey and Mary Finan. Brilliant people one and all. My mates from school were there too: Dave Burke, Jason Stubbs and John Connolly. As luck would have it, the guys were there to provide the evening's entertainment for the night as Pay Back, an excellent covers band. They reminded me of the importance of spending time with people who actually fill your cup of positivity, not drain it.

In October 2007, I was privileged to attend the Cauldwell Extreme Project Conference in Dingle, where I finally got to meet guys like Pat Falvey, Mick Murphy, Emma Carroll and the three Irish doctors, including Dr Roger McMarrow, who took part in the May study on Everest. It was wonderful to hear the talk Dr Mike Grocott gave; it was a truly inspiring and touching presentation. We all sat there in awe. It was the first time the whole challenge of Everest had been put into some kind context for me by other climbers.

My passion for life and those in my life had retuned. A really good pal of mine, Alana Durak, whom I've known since she was a kid, was on the phone the other day to touch base. Her mum, Tish, has been a good friend since our involvement with Aware Defeat Depression.

Alana had decided to run her first marathon and, despite having literally no iron in her blood and a haemoglobin count of less than ten, she ran an incredible time of less than three hours and thirty minutes. We all know amazing, incredible people like Alana, like my godson Seany, or nephew Andrew, or my own wonderful parents and sister Denise, all of whom, for different reasons have inspired me each and every day of my life.

I have now learned so many important things – not least the need to always be proud of your achievements and of who you are.

ひひひ

I know you have two questions on your mind at this point.

Did I contact my birth father? Yes, I did. I've written a letter to him. Life is short and it isn't a dress rehearsal, right? Besides, if one of his other children was to announce that they wanted to climb to the roof of the word, I thought he might appreciate some advice…

And, secondly, would I go back? Only a fool would answer that question.

Looking to the future, what's next for me? I don't know the answer to that. But there are other things I would like to do – namely, to settle down and have at least one child. All of you reading this who have children should be smug knowing that I went around the world to discover that what I really want in life is to be a father. As for what challenges lie ahead. *Poli poli*, as my Tanzanian friends would say. One step at a time.

I hope you all enjoy your trip up your own mountains. We are all so anxious to be at the top that we forget to admire the view on the way up. Take the time to look around you as you fight for that promotion, await the birth of your child or strive to be the best that you can be. Goal set through; there's always something else to strive for. Appreciate the factors that will inspire you to get there – be that music, sport, your own environment – but, most of all, appreciate the people around you. Take comfort in the wonderful people you know and allow them fill your cup every day. When you struggle for inspiration, look around you at the people in this world, some better off, some not, but each with something to give. Goal set for life, not just for work and remember to polish your heart every single day. You must be proud of the person you are before others can fully appreciate your wonder. I may be broke, I may be single, but I have never been happier or prouder, for all that I am, and all that I continue to strive to be every single day. Live in the middle of the now and always remember that real success should be measured by living the life that you want to live.